Called to
Holy
Worldliness

Laity Exchange Books
Mark Gibbs, General Editor

Called to Holy Worldliness

Richard J. Mouw

FORTRESS PRESS   Philadelphia

LAITY EXCHANGE BOOKS

Library of Congress Cataloging in Publication Data

Mouw, Richard J
Called to holy worldliness.

(Laity exchange books)
Bibliography: p.
1. Laity. 2. Christian life—1960–
I. Title. II. Series.
BV4525.M64   262'.15   80-8047
ISBN 0-8006-1397-X

8526F80   Printed in the United States of America   1–1397

Contents

Editor's Introduction

WHY HAS the so-called lay movement in the churches—which seemed strong in the 1950s—moved so slowly? Why are so many Christian laity still so weak in their commitment and so confused about their responsibilities? Certainly, there have been notable advances in almost all the churches, from Roman Catholics to Baptists, in the theological understanding of the common vocation under God of all Christian people, both laity and clergy, both men and women, regardless of age or class or education or race or nationality. And yes, in some aspects of our common discipleship—for instance, in our personal and family relationships—we can see distinct progress in understanding and in sensitivity. But, even in the 1980s, many lay people in many churches feel that their understanding of their Christian calling is uncertain and that their relationships with the clergy are unsatisfactory. We are still a long way from the vision that the 99 percent of God's people—the laity—shall be as effective as Christians as the 1 percent of ordained clergy, that we in our lives and jobs shall see God's will for us as clearly as clergy seem to do for their particular work and responsibilities.

One of the main reasons why things have moved slowly is a lack of hard thinking about our proper role as laity, both in the church and in the world. Even now, many of the growing stream of conferences and congresses for the laity, many of the programs to get us "socially involved," and even a good many of the books and materials in print do not seem to go far beyond "chapter 1." They repeat the insights of past years; they call us to our tremendous responsibilities; but they do not give us much more to chew on. This is why the Audenshaw Foundation (which employs me), together with our good friends at the Vesper Society of San Leandro, California, have started a new mailing service called *Laity Exchange,* which helps both formal and informal church organizations to exchange information about the laity and about models of laity education and development. We have been much encouraged by the fact that *Laity Exchange* has already gained some thirty-five sponsors from different denominations and agencies, both in North America and in Europe.

Now we are able to take another step forward. Here is the first of a new series of *Laity Exchange Books,* which are specifically designed to help Christian people, both laity and clergy, to think further about the calling and the responsibilities of the laity today. We shall concentrate particularly on the life and witness of lay people in the world, in their work and politics and leisure. It gives me very great pleasure to introduce this first book in the series by Professor Richard Mouw, especially as he comes from a strong evangelical tradition. I have always felt that other Christians have underestimated the potential of evangelicals in developing laity concerns. Admittedly, some of us have felt uneasy about certain styles in evangelism and certain tendencies to a purely personal and "otherworldly" piety. But one of the great strengths of evangelicals is that they have always acknowledged the great call of our Lord to *all* his people. They have taken seriously the doctrine of the "priesthood of all believers."

And now, returning to the best traditions of the evangelicals of the past, they are increasingly determined to develop not only a high standard of personal behavior, but also an understanding of the social and public implications of the gospel. Professor Mouw has been a strong leader in these new developments among North American evangelicals. His personal belief in the Lordship of Jesus Christ and his determination to respect and to make clear the biblical message for our times has produced reflections that will surely make us—from whatever Christian tradition we come—think very hard indeed about the world we live in and our responsibilities in it.

MARK GIBBS

Preface

I AM a lay person because of a very conscious choice. As a high school student I decided that I wanted to become an ordained minister. Although I became less firm in that desire during my college years, I did enter a theological seminary after graduation. After two years of seminary study, I dropped out to pursue a career as a college teacher.

I have never regretted my decision to live out my life as a member of the laity. This is not to deny that I suffered, in earlier years, from occasional bouts of guilt and discomfort about abandoning plans to pursue what I had long considered to be the "highest" of Christian callings. But the more I have reflected on what it means to be "laity," the more convinced I have become that the ministries available to lay persons as they pursue their callings outside the walls of the institutional church are at least as exciting, and are at least as deserving of being called "ministry," as those tasks associated with the ordained pastorate.

I became very self-consciously interested in "laity issues" as a result of a conference on "The Laity—A New Direction," held at the University of Dallas in June 1976. As a speaker at that conference I was challenged to relate many of the matters about which I had been writing and lecturing—evangelism, Christianity and politics, Christian social action—in an explicit way to the "theology of the laity" as developed by Hendrick Kraemer, Yves Congar, and others. At that conference I was introduced to a network of individuals, including Howard Blake, Mark Gibbs, Joseph Gremillion, Cynthia Wedel, and Hans-Ruedi Weber, who have been deeply committed to consciousness raising among, and on behalf of, the laity. These concerns were reinforced by my subsequent membership on the continuing steering committee of "The Laity—A New Direction" and on the editorial board of *Laity Exchange*.

This book has grown out of an attempt to take those concerns and involvements seriously. In writing it, I have been motivated by at least three factors that bear mentioning here at the outset of the discussion. The first is a desire to address issues that belong to what my friend and editor Mark Gibbs calls "chapter two" of a theology of the laity. It is time to go "beyond Kraemer." There has been much talk in recent years about how the laity are really, after all, the people of God, and how the church hierarchies must be sensitive to laity concerns, and how we ought not to promote "clericalism," and so on. There has been a widespread insistence that the laity do have very important ministries to carry out in the world. Of course, all this talk has not always been "taken" very well. But there has at least been talk of this sort.

Very little has been said, however, about how the laity ought to go about structuring and carrying out their ministries in the world. This is the stuff of "chapter two" in laity theology. But I must quickly add that this book just barely gets into "chapter two." It certainly does not go on to "chapter three" issues, in which very nitty-gritty "how to" questions would be addressed. Those looking for *very* practical advice will find this book disappointing. But I do hope that many readers will be helped by this attempt to take one step beyond a mere repetition of the fundamentals of laity theology.

A second concern has been to write a book addressed to an ecumenical audience. This is not an easy assignment for me. I am accustomed to writing to "conservative evangelical" audiences in general and Calvinist ones in particular. In writing this book, I have tried to keep reminding myself that I must make my meaning clear to Methodists and Lutherans, Mennonites and Baptists, Eastern Orthodox and Roman Catholics. Whether I have succeeded is a matter for readers to judge.

Third, I have tried to write for the "average church member" and not for academics or clergy. I do not mean "average church member" to be a derogatory term. In my view of the laity, which should be clear in the discussion that follows, I have a very special place for the "worldly" laity—those lay persons who are pursuing Christian ministry beyond the walls of the institutional church. From this perspective a person might be only "average" as a church member, but very special and unique as an agent of the kingdom of Jesus in the world.

During the past several years I have had occasion to give talks, in some cases series of talks, to a number of adult education classes in local congregations and to other groups whose members are primarily lay people. I am very much indebted to those audiences for their questions and criticisms—all of which helped to shape the discussion that takes place in this book. At a few points I have also drawn on articles I wrote for *The Reformed Journal* and *Laity Exchange*.

I owe a special word of thanks to the editor of this series, Mark Gibbs. His encouragement and advice have been extremely valuable to me in pursuing this project, and his editorial scrutiny of my manuscript saved me from committing a number of errors and infelicities.

All quotations from the Bible in my discussion are, unless noted otherwise in the text, taken from the Revised Standard Version.

RICHARD J. MOUW

A Corporate Calling

IN THE SPRING of 1976 I boarded a plane in Newark, New Jersey, on my way to Texas. I sat next to a rather dignified Texas gentleman, and, as we waited for takeoff, we began to talk. "Texas is a pretty exciting place to be this week," he observed. It was the presidential primary season, and the Texas primary elections were coming up in a week. The Texan went on, "This is going to be a good election for us. We're going to win this one!" I cautiously inquired about the identity of the "we." "Reagan," he replied. "I'm in oil, and Reagan is for oil. So oil is for Reagan."

It was too early in the day for political debate, so I offered a noncommittal "uh-huh" and quickly got back to the mystery novel I was reading. The plane took off. After we were in the air, the gentleman pulled down the seat tray and began working on some materials he retrieved from his briefcase. Out of the corner of my eye I noticed that he was working with a Bible and a legal pad.

He read and took notes for several minutes and then leaned back in his seat. After a brief silence he tapped my arm. "Young man, you probably won't understand why I have to say this, but I want to apologize for what I said back there on the runway. You see, I'm a Christian, and I teach an adult Sunday school class at my church. This Sunday I have to talk to my class about the Epistle of James. That's a book in the Bible that says a lot about God's concern for the poor. We Christians have been learning a lot about that subject lately. Jesus cares about the poor, and so I have to also. Now when I listen to these candidates I can't help noticing that Reagan doesn't say much about the poor. Some of the other candidates do; they sound like Jesus when they talk about the poor. So I've made a deal with the Lord: in the primary I'm going to vote oil, but in the general election I'm going to vote Jesus!"

I assured him that I did indeed understand what he was talking about, and we had a fine conversation together about biblical matters. We talked very little about Carter and Reagan and the other candidates, but we had a fascinating conversation about the complexities of Christian discipleship. What impressed me most about this Christian gentleman was his basic posture of openness to the biblical message. He did not have all his ideas and convictions tied together in the form of a coherent theology. (Neither do I.) But I was impressed by his struggle. He was beginning to sense that his Savior went with him into the voting booth. He knew that there had to be some connections between what he said in Sunday school and the political opinions he expressed on airplanes.

Looking for the Connections

This man is not alone in developing these convictions and sensitivities. He is one of a growing number of Christians—Baptist, Episcopalian, Methodist, Roman Catholic, Eastern Orthodox—in North America, Europe, and the Third World who are asking, "What does the gospel mean for my involvement in the political arena?"

But my fellow traveler's comments also reveal something about the stage at which many lay Christians are in their present struggles. He knew that the gospel meant something for his voting patterns; he was clear about the fact that the connection must be made. But he had not yet begun to think much about what his Christian commitment meant for the basic patterns of his business involvement. "Oil" and "Jesus" stood side by side in his mind. Each was making political demands on him, and each set of demands had to be accommodated—a "deal" must be made.

An alternative picture is one in which Jesus is Lord over both business and politics. Our involvement in "oil," too, must be brought into obedience to the rule of Jesus. But, of course, this approach raises significant difficulties. It is one thing to cast a vote as a Christian; it is quite another to attempt to bring the full range of our business and professional activity into conformity with Christian principles.

I do not mean to imply that the gentleman from Texas never thought about the need to be a Christian in his business activities. If he is anything like other devout Christian business people with whom I have talked, he undoubtedly has. But I find that many such people limit their concerns to personal dealings within their business lives. They attempt to be truthful with colleagues, employees, and customers. They work hard and long, seeking to earn an "honest dollar." And they draw on the resources of their personal faith so as to conduct themselves personally in a proper Christian manner.

Consider the way one businessman put it recently: "I don't know how I would survive in the dog-eat-dog world of business if I couldn't regularly get away from it all to spend some time with the Lord." There is nothing intrinsically wrong with this kind of testimony. Christianity is, among other things, a personal religion, and there is nothing silly or wrongheaded about discussing it in very personal terms. The gospel of Jesus Christ does provide us with "inner resources"; it does offer "peace" in the midst of difficult circumstances.

Problems arise, however, when this kind of testimony is offered as a final or overall account of the relationship between Christianity and business activity. This way of looking at things leaves many important issues untouched. Granted that my Christian faith can offer me peace of heart in the midst of the "dog-eat-dog" world of business, but what does it say *to* that world? What does it say about the "dog-eat-dog" patterns themselves? If Christianity offers peace to us when we "get away from it all," does it also say something about the "it all" that we have to get back to?

There are questions that have to be asked about our involvement in the structures, the corporate life of human society. These are difficult questions, as we shall see in proceeding with our discussion. But the questions cannot be avoided, because they are crucial to an understanding of what it means to be God's people in the contemporary world.

And the questions are, properly understood, unavoidable. We cannot escape them by insisting that we are not "into social action." They are not questions that can be left for specialists to consider, nor are they the exclusive concern of "liberals" and "right-wingers" and "liberation theologians." They are questions that must be dealt with by all Christians who are consumers, wage earners, parents, church members, and citizens.

Theology and Corporate Concerns

For one thing, questions about our involvement in the corporate life of human society—business, politics, entertainment, education—are intimately related to theological concerns. To see this, we do not have to look any farther than the First Article of the Apostles' Creed, where we confess that God is "Maker of heaven and earth." Christians are committed to a doctrine of creation. We believe that the world and all that is in it are not the product of chance but result from the creative activity of God.

Some Christians have understood the doctrine of creation in such a way that they are opposed to various kinds of "evolutionary" teachings. Thus, fundamentalist Christians have been willing to expend much time, energy, and money attempting to ban public school textbooks that present only an evolutionary perspective; they conduct these battles out of a professed adherence to a theology of "special creation."

What strikes me as odd is that many of these same defenders of divine creation have been noticeably silent about the battle against racism. For racism is also a denial of "special creation." Racism is among other things a theological heresy. It denies that all human beings are created in God's image. It is odd that Christians, who are very much concerned about textbooks that deny a certain understanding of creation, are so silent about social systems that treat black schoolchildren as if they were mere pawns in an evolutionary struggle.

A proper theology of creation must also take into account human uses and allocations of the natural resources God has created. What does a theology of creation have to say about a nation whose nuclear stockpile can destroy the entire population of the world twelve times over? What does it say about the way we mine minerals, pump and use oil, build and run machines? What does it say about recycling bottles and cans? What are the implications of the biblical teaching regarding creation for the way in which we farm and garden, eat meals, and entertain ourselves?

Or take our Christian belief in "one holy Catholic church." To utter this confession is to express solidarity with millions of black Christians in South Africa whose abilities to function as Christian worshipers, workers, and families are severely hampered by racist laws. Christians who live under Marxist and right-wing dictatorships are being imprisoned because of their faith in Jesus Christ. Any Christian who professes to believe in the universality and oneness of the body of Christ simply must think of the implications of this profession for our attitudes toward international relations and trade. I do not mean to imply that we ought to be concerned only about the plight of Christians. But I am suggesting that even if we could think of no other reason to show an interest in situations in which human rights are violated, we could be compelled to do so by our doctrine of the church.

Piety and Corporate Concerns

A concern for corporate human life relates not only to our theology, but also to our piety. I am using the word *piety* here in a positive sense. Originally, it connoted "godliness" or "reverence," which is close to the sense I intend. Our patterns of piety have to do with the ways in which we cultivate and express our religious attitudes; these patterns include our personal devotional practices, the ways in which we pray and sing, and the means we employ to talk about our Christian faith.

When I was growing up in "conservative evangelical" circles, there was an illustration that was often used by preachers and evangelists. It went like this: Imagine a scholar teaching today at a well-known university, who is the world's leading expert on the political career of Abraham Lincoln. He knows everything there is to know from scholarly sources about Lincoln. Mention any week during the War Between the States and this scholar can tell you what was occupying Lincoln's thoughts during that week. He has memorized many of Lincoln's speeches, and he can discuss at length the major and minor political decisions made by Lincoln during his career.

And now, the illustration continued, imagine a little girl who actually lived next door to Mr. Lincoln. Each day she would see Lincoln. He would pick her up and hold her in his arms. He would whisper a secret in her ear; sometimes he might read her a story or tell her a joke.

The punch line of this illustration inevitably came in the form of what was intended as a rhetorical question: which person knows Lincoln better? The man who knows many facts about Lincoln, but who does not know him personally, or the little girl Lincoln counted as a personal friend? Of course, it was expected that we would all agree that the little girl knew Lincoln better.

There is a legitimate point to that illustration, which I do not mean to deny. But it is also a misleading example. Consider an analogous situation. Imagine a reporter at a large city newspaper who is an expert on the career of a certain leading figure in organized crime. This reporter knows all that there is to learn from the public record about this criminal. He knows the extent of his legal and illegal business ventures. He knows everything about all the murders for which he is responsible. He knows much about the man's struggle to gain ascendency in the sordid world of organized crime. But he has never met the man personally.

Now imagine a little girl who lives next door to this criminal figure. Each day when he sees her, he picks her up and holds her in his arms. Sometimes he whispers a secret into her ear; or he tells her a joke or a story.

Which person knows the criminal figure better? It isn't at all obvious that we would insist that the little girl has the edge in this situation. She knows the gangster personally. But she does not know much *about* him. She does not know about the nature of his activities, the extent of his perverse dealings. The reporter does know these things.

The point of the Lincoln example was obviously to say something about our relationship to Jesus Christ. It was a means of illustrating the need to know him "personally," to know him as a Savior of souls, as a kindly shepherd. But the gangster example points to a somewhat misleading element in this kind of emphasis. Sometimes we do not really "know" a person unless we know many things *about* that person.

This has application to our understanding of what proper Christian piety is. The development of patterns of piety is often stressed as a substitute for concern about the corporate dimensions of human life. A few years ago I attended a gathering of Roman Catholic charismatics, and I heard someone put the case this way: "Before I received the Holy Spirit, I was the kind of Catholic who worried all of the time about political and economic issues. But now that I'm Spirit-filled, I let others worry about those things. I'm just too busy getting to know Jesus better!''

This testimony betrays a widespread misunderstanding of pious growth. Many Christians who stress the development of a ''personal relationship with Jesus Christ''—an emphasis common to many manifestations of ''pietism'' in the history of Christianity—understand Christian growth in *intensive* terms. ''Getting to know Jesus better'' means getting to feel increasingly ''warmer'' about Jesus; it is to develop more and more intensive *feelings* about him.

This ignores the *extensive* dimensions of growth. To grow in the knowledge of Christ is also to grow in our grasp of the *extent* of his power. The Bible uses a variety of terms and titles to refer to Jesus' relationship to his followers. As ''Savior'' or ''Shepherd'' he cares for us, nourishes us, bathes us in his love. But he is also ''Lord,'' and this refers to his disciplining power, to his authority in our lives. And he is ''King''—a title that refers to the very real authority Jesus exercises over all other authorities, whether political, economic, familial, or educational. Our piety—the prayers we use, the songs we sing, the language of our confession and testimony—is filled with these many terms and titles. So, often our piety commits us to more than we are aware of when we speak of our relationship to Jesus Christ.

A while ago I was asked to speak at a midweek Lenten service at a large suburban church. The minister who invited me asked me to speak about the political dimensions of the ministry of Jesus, but he warned me, ''My people are pretty conservative. They don't think Christianity has anything to do with politics. Lay it on them, but be aware of where they're at.'' The service began with the congregation singing ''O Worship the King.'' And then the children's choir sang ''Jesus loves the little children . . ./red and yellow, black and white,/ they are precious in his sight.'' When I began to speak, I pointed out to the congregation that my basic premise had already been established by them: Jesus is political. They had addressed him as ''King'' in their opening hymn; and the children had testified to the fact that little black and red and yellow children are precious in the sight of King Jesus. The only issues about ''Christianity and politics'' that remained to be dealt with were: What are we going to do about the connections we have already established in our piety? What does King Jesus think about napalm? Or about ghetto housing? Or about life in reservations and barrios? And what are we going to do to be obedient to his political designs?

Many Christians, of course, are inattentive to the substance of their own piety. When they refer to Jesus as "King" or "Judge," they intend these terms as mere metaphors. The terms function as metaphorical compliments being paid to Jesus; they are poetic ways of telling Jesus that he is very important. But this is to rob the titles of their biblical content. When the early Christians confessed that "Jesus is Lord," this was meant as a rejection of all claims by human political rulers to supreme "lordship." When the Apostle John, a political exile on the island of Patmos, described Jesus as "the ruler of kings on earth" (Rev. 1:5), he was referring to the actual authority Jesus exercises over corrupt kings and princes.

We need to reflect on the content of our expressions of piety, to see what our utterances implicitly and explicitly commit us to. This is an important requirement for getting ourselves, as Christian laity, to understand the scope of our corporate calling. The task is not so much for us to *begin* saying new things; rather, it is to begin to reflect and act on the commitments we have made in the expressions of piety, the hymns and prayers with which we are already familiar.

Evangelism and Corporate Concern

Responsibility for the corporate patterns of human life is also intimately related to the task of evangelism. It is unfortunate that in some Christian circles evangelism is treated as something very different from "social action." It is even more unfortunate that some Christians insist on choosing *for* evangelism *against* engagement in social action. Someone put the case this way in a recent conversation: "I suppose that there is some room for Christians to wrestle with social issues. But that's not my choice. I see my calling as one of engaging in evangelism. I'll spend my time winning souls for Christ; social action is something I'll leave to the liberals."

This "evangelism versus social action" view can be sustained only where people have a very narrow understanding of both the scope and the target population of evangelistic activity. The scope of evangelism can be expressed in rather simple terms: evangelism is the spreading of the good news about Jesus Christ. But the good news is a very complex story. In Luke's account of Jesus' early ministry, Jesus himself gives a rather "social" account of the good news:

> The Spirit of the Lord is upon me,
> because he has anointed me to preach good news to the poor.
> He has sent me to proclaim release to the captives
> and recovering of sight to the blind,
> to set at liberty those who are oppressed,
> to proclaim the acceptable year of the Lord.
>
> (Luke 4:18–19)

We will return further on to the relationship between the gospel and the poor and oppressed. Suffice it here to mention the fact that the Scriptures regularly designate the gospel as "good news for the poor."

In considering the scope of the gospel, we must also think about what properly goes into "spreading" the good news. Many recent studies of evangelism have stressed the unity of "word" and "deed" in the work of evangelism—and rightly so. It is not enough to talk about Christianity. Spreading the good news must also involve us in demonstrating the implications of the Christian message. Matthew's version of Jesus' Great Commission to his disciples is instructive here (Matt. 28:18–20). The command to "make disciples of all nations, baptizing them" is bracketed on either side by items that are often ignored in discussions of evangelism and missions. This command is prefaced by the reminder that "all authority in heaven and on earth has been given to" Jesus, and it is immediately followed by the instruction that converts are to be taught "to observe all that I have commanded you." Evangelism is done in the name of him who holds supreme authority in heaven and on earth, and it includes the mandate to teach all the commandments of Jesus.

Evangelism must include presenting good news to the poor. It must be done in the name of the One who is King over all things. It must involve both verbal witness and exemplary deeds. It must bring the full gospel to the whole person.

Many of these same concerns arise in considering the target population toward whom evangelistic efforts are directed. People who prefer "evangelizing" to "social action" often manage to do so only because they restrict their evangelistic efforts to the white middle class.

It may be possible to ignore "social issues" while conducting neighborhood evangelism in the suburbs, or while passing out religious literature in business districts; but to evangelize in the ghettos, or on reservations—while attending to the actual needs of those who are being evangelized—will inevitably force an address to the social, economic, and political environment.

Suppose we attempt to pass out Bibles or religious literature among poverty-stricken blacks in a major city. Many of them will not be able to read our literature. If we investigate why this is so, we must acknowledge the fact that a great number of them have been provided with only an inferior education. This, in turn, has something to do with city budgets and political representation. We will also encounter low self-images brought about by desperate poverty or dependence on government programs. We must further contend with the fact that the black family in North America has been under systematic attack, first by the slavery system and more recently by the welfare system and chronic unemployment. And, of course, underlying all of this are the brutal realities of racism.

If we are going to evangelize *in* that situation, *to* that situation—if we are going to attempt to present good news to living, breathing, hurting human beings who are weighed down by a multifaceted oppression—we cannot avoid "social issues."

A number of studies of plantation slavery in the United States note that slave owners were often very nervous about attempts on the part of churches, white and black, to evangelize black slaves. Their nervousness related to two problems. For one thing, the evangelists themselves often became very critical of slavery in the process of attempting to "win souls." It was difficult to approach the slave with a genuine desire to see that person accept the claims of the gospel and not become very sensitive to the dehumanizing conditions that were part and parcel of plantation slavery. A second problem was that the gospel tended to reinforce the slaves' discontent with their condition. This often happened in very practical ways: the slaves cultivated a desire to learn to read, they wanted a stable family life, they wanted places of worship constructed. But most of all, they discovered the gospel's offer of freedom, an offer that they had difficulty distinguishing from the hope for freedom from physical enslavement.

Evangelism cannot be divorced from social, political, and economic change, especially when it takes place among the oppressed. Even where those who evangelize are not aware of the corporate implications of their own message, those implications are not lost on those who come to accept the gospel through their agency.

There is no way, then, that Christians can escape from a concern for the corporate dimensions of human life—from social, political, economic, and ecological concerns. If we begin with doctrine or theology, we find that very basic theological formulas have clear implications for corporate life, for the structures of human society. If we begin with personal or group piety, we discover that the expressions of our piety commit us to a concern for social structures. If we attempt to avoid "social concerns" by committing ourselves to programs of evangelism, we will discover that we cannot ultimately avoid corporate concerns.

It should be clear by now what all of this means for a proper understanding of the nature and calling of the laity. The laity has a ministry to conduct in society; we are called to engage in what some have called a "ministry to the structures of society."

Many Callings

Before pursuing our discussion of the nature of this ministry any further, two points of clarification should be appended to this contention that we must engage in a ministry to structures. The first point is that I do not mean to imply that this is our *only* ministry. We must be very suspicious of any claim that would attempt to delineate what *the* calling of the laity (or of the church, or of the Christian) is. The New Testament community of the people of God has many callings, many ministries. Another way of putting this is to say that we have a multidimensional ministry or calling.

The fundamentalists sing a little song that goes, "Saved, saved, to tell others." Strictly speaking, this is inaccurate. The whole of the Christian calling cannot be subsumed under the category of "personal evangelism"—nor can it be subsumed under "ministry to social structures." These categories point to *dimensions* of the overall mission of the people of God—and important dimensions at that. But no single formula of this sort captures the whole picture. We are called as a people to celebrate God's mighty deeds, to grow in grace as individuals and communities, to *be* model communities in the world, to bear one another's burdens, to pray, to heal bodies, to comfort the bereaved, and so on.

The second point follows from this first one. It would be wrong to insist that everyone must share, in the same way and to the same degree, in a ministry to social structures. This is a dangerous point to insist on, because many Christians would love to seize on any means for escaping their responsibilities in this area. But truthfulness and clarity require that the point be made nevertheless. For one thing, there are Christians who cannot be expected to have any share in such a ministry. Peter Berger made this point effectively in the early 1960s, in the course of discussing the need for a radical reform of congregational life:

> [T]here are many of the aged and the sick and the emotionally crippled in our congregations to whom these radical calls for institutional revolution can mean nothing but a threat to whatever spiritual solace the congregation has been able to give them. There is every reason to speak of the vocation of Christians in industrial society, for instance. But there are some Christians whose one vocation remains to suffer and to face death in faith. It is certainly no minor accomplishment if a local congregation provides the communal support for such a vocation. Such accomplishment is unspectacular and very unrevolutionary, but it is enough to forbid the assumption that *only* in radical new forms can the Church perform a witness.
>
> *(The Noise of Solemn Assemblies,* page 170)

Berger's point is well taken. And if it is true that there are some lay people who have virtually no personal mandate to minister to social structures, it is also true that the rest of the laity will be involved in such a ministry in varying degrees.

It would be both theologically and pastorally defective to begin by imposing specific obligations—e.g., the obligation to engage in corporate witness—on each individual lay person. The place to begin is with the overall calling of the community of the people of God. This community, as we have already indicated, has a complex, multi-dimensional calling. And one of its obligations, one dimension of its calling, is to engage in a ministry to, or within, social structures.

Having begun with a clear understanding of the corporate calling of the community, we must stress that the task of each individual is to discern how he or she can participate in that overall calling of the community. The comments we have just made about persons who may be completely exempted from that task, or who may be only minimally involved in that task, have to be taken seriously. But it must also be stressed that, for all practical purposes, to take the corporate calling of the people of God as a clear obligation will have the effect of getting many of us *more* involved, and not less so. Berger's observation that there are some Christians whose single calling is to die gracefully is correct; but there are not many able-bodied lay persons who fall under this category.

2

Theology and the Laity

JUST ABOUT any discussion of the laity will point out that our word apparently comes from the Greek word *laos,* which is used in the Bible (in both the Septuagint and the New Testament) to refer to the "people" of God. In a strict etymological sense, then, every member of the church—ordained or nonordained—is a member of the laity.

But the word has come to have a somewhat narrower meaning. As things developed in the history of the Christian church, "laity" came to be a term of contrast with "clergy." In my use of the term *laity* I will be following this historical usage rather than what is often taken to be the literal meaning of the term, but with some qualifications: historically the laity have sometimes been understood to constitute a class that is both different from, and inferior to, the clergy. In using the term, I mean to acknowledge the difference but not the allegedly inferior status.

I am aware of the fact that some readers will resent this use of the term *laity.* Recently, I heard a strong objection expressed along these lines: "To refer to 'laity' and 'clergy' is to foster an unbiblical dualism. We are all members of the *laos,* God's people. We must not give the impression that there is a deep divide between the ordained and the nonordained members of the community of the people of God."

It is not difficult to appreciate these sentiments. But the fact is that there are important differences between the ordained and the nonordained. At least, there are important differences between those who work full-time as salaried employees of the institutional church and those of us who spend most of our working hours outside of that institution. These differences, as I see things, are to be neither ig-

nored nor regretted. There are, of course, other actual differences
between the ordained and the nonordained that are regrettable and
ought to be abolished. But until they are abolished we ought not to
ignore the realities of the situation. My use of the term *laity* in this
discussion is meant as a way of acknowledging the facts of life in the
Christian community. As things currently stand, if such a term did not
exist, we would have to invent it.

Patterns of Discrimination

It would be an understatement to say that the Christian laity have
not always fared well in the church. Throughout church history the
laity—or some significant portion of the laity—have consistently
come out on the short end of some comparison or another. There have
been periods in which "the laity" has, for all practical purposes, if not
in principle, been distinguished from "the church"—where the latter
term was used to refer to the ordained leadership of the institutional
church. And even when the term *church* was used to cover both
clergy and laity, lay persons were often treated as the weaker partner
in the relationship.

These ancient patterns of discrimination have not disappeared
completely; indeed, they can often be found today existing in pure
form. But in recent times at least two other sorts of discriminatory
ways of viewing matters have emerged. One is a perspective wherein
the laity itself is split into two groups. Mark Gibbs and T. Ralph
Morton have drawn attention to this way of viewing the situation in
their discussion of the distinction between the "churchy" laity and
the "worldly" laity *(God's Frozen People,* page 23.) The churchy
laity are those who are willing to commit much time and energy to
maintaining the institutional church; they function in various church
offices and/or serve in the choirs, the church educational programs,
and in various church-related societies and organizations. These lay
persons are often dear to the hearts of the clergy; they are the ones
who regularly receive praise as "active laity."

The worldly laity are those who perceive their primary Christian
calling as taking place in the context of their daily work, beyond the
borders of the institutional church. Often they have a sincere desire
to allow their Christian commitment to influence their "secular"
activities.

Gibbs and Morton are quite correct in noting that the worldly laity are often discriminated against by the ecclesiastical establishment—the "really involved" laity are regularly identified by church leaders as those who are preoccupied with churchy activities. A few years ago I read in a church periodical a tribute to a layman who had died recently. This person had been extremely active in many areas of his chosen profession, and he consistently viewed his daily work as a form of Christian ministry. The tribute listed his professional accomplishments and then added: "But in all of this he did not neglect his Christian duties." The account went on to note that he had served on several church committees. Whether intentionally so or not, this kind of narrow identification of "Christian duties" with church activities often serves to intimidate those lay people who are inclined to view their primary mission as one of serving Christ in the performance of worldly functions.

More recently, however, the church has begun to devote more explicit attention to equipping the worldly laity for their ministry in society. But even here we can detect at times a distinction that, if carried to extremes, can be dangerous. Unfortunately, the attention is often focused exclusively on equipping "the decision makers" for ministry in the world. The publicity surrounding a recent "congress of the laity" was permeated with this theme: the impression was given that the "real" laity are politicians, football coaches, bank presidents, corporate executives, orchestra conductors, and others of that ilk. Little attention was given to the callings of the waitress, the water boy, the telephone operator, the third-chair violinist, the clerk in the florist shop, or the parent whose primary task is managing a home.

Equipping All the Laity

There is, of course, much to be said in favor of a specific address to laity who are in positions of power in various prominent institutions. They have special opportunities and special problems, and their unique needs must be considered (as they will be in another book in this Laity Exchange series, *Christians with Secular Power,* by Mark Gibbs). But these needs must not be emphasized to the exclusion of other segments of the laity. If we were to overcome past biases against the laity as such, or against the worldly laity, only to show favoritism to the rich and powerful lay people, we would not have solved the problem of exclusiveness, which has plagued discussions of the role of the laity for centuries.

Furthermore, discrimination against the laity, or certain subgroups thereof, is closely interwoven with other patterns of discrimination within the Christian community. Indeed, I am tempted at times to argue that the question of the nature and role of the laity is *the* fundamental question to be faced by the church today, and that other important issues are, in fact, variations on this issue. This may be to state the case too strongly. But the question of the laity does intersect in significant ways with other crucial issues.

Take the question of the role of women in the church. Given the practical realities of church life, the question of ordaining women has at least two crucial dimensions: not only do many Christians have a much too "low" view of women; they also have a much too "high" a view of the ordained ministry. The gap, then, between women and ordination is twice widened. And even when some women make it across this double divide, we have not yet dealt with the powerlessness of those Christians who are not only women but also laity.

Or take the concern for granting power to racial minorities within the church. It is difficult enough for blacks and Hispanics and native Americans to function in the context of predominantly white churches; but the problems are greatly compounded when one is a black or Hispanic or native American *lay* person.

Lest I be misunderstood on these matters, I must stress my support for the efforts of women and racial minorities to gain power within the present ecclesiastical structures. But the success of those efforts will leave some crucial concerns untouched. Ultimately, the solution is not to allow some members of presently powerless groups to enter into an elite, powerful group; the problem of elitism as such in the church must be addressed.

But is it really proper to talk about struggling for "power" in the church? Isn't this a manifestation of a somewhat cynical view of how things get done in the context of the body of Christ? I think not. For one thing legitimate power struggles have taken place many times in the history of the church. In Roman Catholicism the issue of power and factionalism becomes public every time there is a papal election. Most Protestant denominations have their origins in power struggles against entrenched churches of the past. Many of us regularly celebrate heroines and heroes in our own traditions who were willing to throw off various yokes of ecclesiastical bondage in past centuries.

In at least one important sense the church is a "political" organization. Every organized group has a political dimension, insofar as that group has patterns of authority and decision making. The church is an entity in which some people have power over other people: the power to decide policy, make appointments, call meetings, set budgets, allocate funds, and so on. We are not "politicizing" the church, then, when we ask whether the present political patterns are good and fair.

What ought to distinguish Christian "power struggles" from struggles that take place in other contexts, however, is the content that goes into our understanding of the "goodness" and "fairness" of our structures. The reform of Christian structures ought never to be called for on the basis of naive acceptance of passing organizational fads, nor should reform programs be launched simply in the name of "democracy," "efficiency," or "human potential."

But if we must be critical and cautious in accepting proposed bases for institutional change, we must also be critical and cautious in accepting proposed bases for *preserving* the status quo. It is difficult to think of a single social movement—even a single fad—that has come along in recent years that has not posed some important questions to the Christian community. Have we perhaps overintellectualized the Christian story to the detriment of the "feelings" dimension of human experience? In what very basic ways have we refused to allow women to grow in grace and knowledge? To what degree has the Christian church been a racist institution? In what ways have we failed to promote sexual honesty and sexual healing? And so on.

Similarly, I believe that recent interest in the nature and calling of the laity constitutes an important challenge to the Christian community. It is to be hoped that this challenge will not be dealt with by simply giving in to a "laity power" movement. As with the many other challenges being posed to the church, this issue must be dealt with critically, cautiously, and *theologically*.

A Theology of the Laity

In his magnificent little book *A Theology of the Laity,* published in 1958, Hendrik Kraemer complained that theologians either neglect the laity altogether or treat the laity as a topic that is "subsidiary" to other theological issues. The situation has improved somewhat since Kraemer aired that complaint, but matters are not yet the way they ought to be. There is still a great need for extensive discussion of the nature and role of the laity.

The required theological discussion must encompass at least three aspects. First, we must develop a more adequate theology *of* the laity. We need careful theologizing about who the laity are in the Christian scheme and what their calling is, or callings are, in the context of the total mission of the Christian community. Rather than having theological discussions in which the laity is a subsidiary topic or a theological afterthought, the standard issues of theological discourse—church, sacraments, mission, salvation, liberation, eschatology, anthropology, "doctrine of God"—must be examined with a central focus on questions concerning the status of the laity.

Strictly speaking, of course, we cannot expect to receive *a* theology of the laity. If the task is taken up throughout the broad Christian community, the result will be a variety of theologies of the laity. This plurality ought to be welcomed. My guess is that significant differences would emerge if we were to see what Roman Catholic, Lutheran, Baptist, Plymouth Brethren, Mennonite, Salvation Army, and African Methodist theologies of the laity would look like. But there might also be significant bases for consensus. The very fact that this requires conjecture as to what *would* happen if such theologies were developed indicates the amount of work remaining to be done in this area.

Second, proper theologizing about the laity must also produce a theology *for* the laity. It must be theological engagement for which the agenda is set by the needs, dilemmas, and problems of the laity. And it must be carried on with the clear goal of building up the laity for their ministries in the world.

Each of these first two dimensions deserves further comment. But some of the issues at stake can be gathered under a third dimension, which is that theological reflection on laity issues must include theology *by* the laity. This may seem to be an odd point to insist on, and it may be that this requirement will have to be modified somewhat. But there is, nonetheless, an important point to be made in this area.

In recent years theologians and other Christian scholars have been engaged in lengthy discussions of the "contextualization" of theology. This notion has been central to recent discussions in theology of missions, or missiology. The emphasis on contextuality points to the fact that theology takes place in specific *contexts*. This may seem like a rather trivial point to make, but in fact it isn't. What is being stressed is the fact that theology takes place in specific cultural, political, and economic contexts and that these contexts profoundly shape the act and the content of theologizing.

It is this recognition that is responsible for the recent introduction of such labels as "black theology" and "feminist theology" into theological discussion, as well as theological perspectives that are self-consciously Latin American, Asian, and African. To put the overall case in rather simple terms, strong arguments are being put forward these days that the kind of theology many of us are used to is too "masculine" in its orientation, too "white" in its fundamental perspective, and too "Western"—or, as some would prefer, too "north Atlantic"—that is, too much molded by Greek philosophical traditions, and too much formed by the economic and political experiences of the dominant social classes.

We have a good deal to learn from those who are lodging these criticisms against theology as it has been formulated in Western societies. Consider briefly one example. Much traditional Western theology has been written by professors working at European universities. Imagine a white male university professor in nineteenth-century Germany who is beginning to write a book about God. Typically, he begins by writing about God's "attributes": God is omnipotent, omniscient, omnipresent, omnibenevolent, and so on.

Now imagine a black slave woman in nineteenth-century North America. As she begins to reflect on and articulate her faith in God, she begins at a very different point. She speaks of a suffering God, a God who identifies with the pain of his oppressed people: "Nobody knows the trouble I've seen, nobody knows but Jesus." The very first thing she thinks to say about God is that he shares in her humiliation; he is acquainted with her grief.

Why the different starting points? Why does the white theologian begin with a God who is in control of things, while the black slave starts with a suffering God? The white theologian is "in control"; the black slave is suffering. Because of their differing contexts, each establishes a different point of contact with the God of the Scriptures.

The contextual nature of theology can be even more obvious than this. It can also be much more subtle. Theologians have begun to explore the subtleties in a careful and systematic manner. There can be no doubt that the universal church is being enriched by these new sensitivities.

It is important to keep in mind, however, that it is not merely being argued that theology *ought* to be contextualized. The contention is that all theology *is* contextualized. It is not that black and feminist and Third World theologians have recently started to contextualize theology. Rather, we are beginning to recognize that the contextualization has been going on all along.

This recognition teaches us something about the diversity of situations in which the gospel has been received. Human beings hear different things in the biblical message, from context to context. The plantation slave, the urban housewife, the Russian peasant, the worker in a rice paddy, the tribal chief—each receives the gospel in terms of contextualized frameworks, questions, and anxieties. To recognize this fact gives new occasion for celebrating the riches, and the universality, of the Christian gospel.

But for some of us, there is also a word of judgment to be heard in this emphasis on contextualization. We have often been closed to other perspectives on the gospel. We have too quickly absolutized the cultural trappings that have accumulated around our understanding of the Christian faith. And this is especially unfortunate for those of us who are white Westerners, because we are, as a group, numbered among the rich and powerful of the earth; we consume a disproportionate amount of the world's goods. And many of us have a degree of control over our own destinies that would be unthinkable in other parts of the world. Unfortunately, this privileged position has influenced the way in which we have received and understood the gospel. We have often filtered out crucial elements of the biblical message. We have often distorted the gospel so as to make it into a message with which we can live comfortably.

But more of this further on in our discussion. For the present we can note that contextualization is also something that takes place *within* groups and cultures, as well as from culture to culture. Even within our own denominations and congregations, there are differing contexts for understanding and appropriating the gospel. This is not to say that the differences within an average North American congregation will be nearly as great as those between that congregation and a group of worshipers in Thailand. But there will be some differences, and they ought not to be ignored.

One such difference—important for our present purposes—is the differing contexts of clergy and laity. And this is an important difference in at least one regard: the theologizing that takes place in the Christian church has been an overwhelmingly *clergy*-oriented activity. Theology has been taught and written by people who are very closely tied to the interests of the clergy; theological issues have been formulated and explored from that point of view, from within that context.

The Laity and Preaching

Am I making much ado over nothing in pointing this out? I think not. Take one area of theology that is very significant for the life of the church: the theology of preaching. An experience I had a few years ago caused me to reflect on this subject. I visited a church one Sunday morning and heard what stands out in my mind as the worst sermon I have ever suffered through. Yet when I left the church, my first reaction was one of guilt. Perhaps I had failed to listen with the proper spirit; maybe I was being overly critical.

The next night I attended a university lecture by a noted visiting historian. His lecture was terrible and everyone knew it. No one, including me, left the lecture hall with the slightest inclination to engage in any soul-searching about the defects in our own moods or attitudes.

Why was going to church different from attending the history lecture? Why shouldn't I have concluded with equal decisiveness in each case that the speaker was at fault and that it would have been best for all of us if we had stayed home? The answer, I think, is that preaching is surrounded with a certain aura that is missing in the case of history lectures. We have a full-fledged *theology* of preaching, something we lack in the area of ordinary lecturing.

In my case the theology of preaching which has influenced me is one that propounds a "high" view of preaching. In this view sermons are very special events. They are occasions in which God speaks to his gathered people through the preacher. The preacher's words are the very words of God, directed toward a specific worshiping congregation.

I do not mean here to submit this view to a systematic theological test. For all I know, this "high" view could ultimately survive such a test as a very plausible theological perspective. But there are nonetheless a number of questions that ought to be asked about it from the perspective of the laity. For example, doesn't such a view perpetuate a very narrow conception of the ways in which God speaks through human beings? The impression given is that God addresses his people exclusively through sermons preached by ordained ministers—that the sermon is a unique and special event in the life of the church. Must things be viewed in this way? Can't, and doesn't, God speak—in the same way as he does in sermons—through the church school teacher, through conversations between Christians over coffee, through parents talking with their children, through Christian activists addressing crucial social issues? Why the special aura surrounding the words of the ordained minister?

And isn't this an unnecessarily intimidating view? Doesn't it put the critical burden on the laity? Doesn't this view function in a way that wards off legitimate criticism of sermons? It serves to place the guilt in the mind of the hearer, even when blame ought properly to be directed toward the speaker.

But most important, who *formulated* this kind of theology about preaching? Books about preaching are almost universally authored by either preachers or teachers of preachers. The same holds for courses on preaching and workshops on preaching. Where are there books by the laity on "how to preach" or on "the nature of preaching"? And why should there not be such books? The sermon is an event in which two parties participate: the one who preaches and those who listen. Why is it that theorizing about preaching is so overwhelmingly weighted on the side of those who preach? Isn't it conceivable that the theology of preaching would have a very different tone and content if it were formulated from the perspective of the laity? Why shouldn't the laity be asked to answer such questions as: What is a sermon? How are we to understand sermons theologically?

In what sense does God speak through sermons? How does the sermon relate to other acts of worship?

Theology by the Laity

This brief foray is merely offered as an example—admittedly one drawn from a tradition that places a central emphasis on the preaching of the Word. But it serves as a case in point for a more general, and thoroughly ecumenical, problem: theology most often reflects the interest and the point of view of the clergy. And this brings us back to the issue originally raised; namely, that we need to have a theological reflection that is carried on *by* the laity.

I am not suggesting that we turn over all chairs of theology to lay persons. Indeed, since my desire is to have the worldly laity engage in theological reflection, it would defeat my purpose if such persons were to become professional theologians—in so doing, they would cease to be worldly laity. What I am suggesting is that we need theology, at least some theology, that is approached from the point of view of the laity; we need theology that reflects the concerns, questions, and interests of those laity who are attempting to function as ministers of Christ in the world.

To speak of a theology *by* the laity, then, is to insist that there be a properly contextualized theology *of* the laity. We would all think it odd if a lifelong resident of Paris wrote a book on how to live the life of discipleship in Latin America, or if a sixty-three-year-old bachelor wrote a book on what it means to experience the Christian faith as a teenage girl. It is, of course, possible that in each case an especially empathetic writer could manage to communicate some profound thoughts on the subject; but it is very unlikely that either person could address the subject in anything like a fully adequate manner. Similarly, there is something odd about an attempt by clergy and professional theologians to speak with authority about the situations faced by mechanics, insurance agents, and farmers. Such attempts may not miss the mark completely, but they are bound to fall short in crucial ways.

And yet these situations must be addressed theologically. There are a number of ways in which theological reflection on such matters can be engaged in by the laity. "By the laity" here does not necessarily

mean that the end theological product must be such that *only* laity
have contributed to that product, but it does mean that the laity must
have a significant role in shaping the product. At the very least, we
must set aside the age-old assumption that adequate theology of, and
for, the laity can be produced without a crucial contribution from
those who experience firsthand the wide variety of contexts in which
the laity find themselves. Further on in the discussion I will make
some concrete proposals concerning how to bring about and utilize
these contributions.

"Anticlericalism"

Some readers may believe that they have detected an "anticlerical" bias in certain of these comments. Before going any further, I
think it important to address this issue. To adapt an old formula: some
of my best friends are members of the clergy. I was raised in a
parsonage, and I attended a seminary for two years before dropping
out to pursue studies in philosophy. I teach at a church college whose
Board of Trustees is made up mainly of clergy. I lecture regularly at
theological seminaries. I conduct workshops and retreats for the
clergy. I preach sermons several times a year.

In short, I am not a very good representative of the worldly laity.
My work and interests regularly intersect with those of the clergy;
indeed, I am often mistaken for a clergyman—during the week in
which I am writing this, I received two letters that prefaced "Rev." to
my name. Even though I am technically a lay person, I am to a
significant degree one of the churchy laity.

But I do speak with some credibility, I think, for the concerns of the
worldly laity. When I went off to secular university campuses for
graduate study in the early 1960s, after six years at church-related
schools, I felt ill prepared for what I encountered. In my efforts to
relate my faith to what I was learning—especially in the areas of
social, political, and economic thought—I was poorly equipped by
my previous Christian training. My evangelical mentors had provided
me with very little that would help me respond, as I felt I must, to
questions about civil rights, poverty, nuclear arms, and the war in
Southeast Asia. As a professor at a Christian liberal-arts college I
must struggle daily with questions and challenges from students who
are on their way to becoming the worldly laity.

I am convinced on the basis of personal experience that the Christian community has often failed—even miserably at times—to equip people who desire to pursue Christian vocations in the world. Some of the responsibility for this failure rests on church leaders, including the clergy. But none of this leads me to adopt a position that could properly be labeled "anticlerical."

One of the more passionate outbreaks of anticlericalism occurred in North America shortly after the American Revolution. Indeed, what occurred then was a series of outbreaks of anticlericalism that took place almost simultaneously in a number of different places. The members of the established clergy were labeled "hireling priests" and "tyrannical oppressors" and were viewed by some as an elitist group intent only on accumulating power and prestige.

It is understandable that some Christians would have carried the revolutionary spirit over into the life of the church in this way, thus issuing their own "declaration of independence" from ecclesiastical control. This is understandable—but not, I think, justified. Similarly, today it is understandable that a disillusionment with bureaucracies and "big government," along with an undercurrent of anti-institutionalism, should result in some animosity toward church leaders. But when this takes the form of anticlericalism, it is not justified.

I am convinced that the Christian church very much needs an educated clergy. This conviction is borne out by the historical development of those groups that came into being out of anticlerical impulses. They gradually developed their own idea of the clergy; and even in those groups that function today without an "official" clergy, we can observe a clear tendency toward singling out certain individuals who perform many of the tasks of the clergy.

This is to be expected. Institutionalization and the development of distinct roles and tasks seem to be an inevitable factor in human groups, and the church is no exception. Furthermore, the church needs leaders who receive the education and resources for building up God's people, who devote considerable time and energy to studying the needs of the flock of God, and who regularly address those needs.

Anticlericalism is, as I see it, wrongheaded. But—and this must be stressed—the proper antidote to anticlericalism is not "pro-clericalism," in the sense of the exaltation or glorification of the clergy. We must recognize the proper place of the clergy; and we must neither overrate nor underrate that place.

The Place of the Clergy

I will not offer here any extensive account of what the proper place of the clergy is. In a sense, of course, the clergy have many "places." In a given congregation the shape of the clergy's work must be decided in the light of several factors. One important consideration has to do with the theological tradition to which the congregation adheres. In some churches sacramental functions will be central; in others, preaching will be crucial; still others may stress a balance between the two. Another consideration will be the needs of the specific congregation; the patterns of clergy leadership in church organizations such as guilds, clubs, and societies will differ from congregation to congregation, as will the need for pastoral counseling, youth work, hospital visitation, and participation in community affairs. A third variable that must be taken into account consists of the gifts and abilities of individual members of the clergy.

We must not, then, underrate the crucial and varied contributions the clergy make to the life of the church. But neither must we overrate the role of the clergy. Misconceptions about the proper place of the clergy in the Christian community often go hand in hand with two confusions. First, we regularly insist that the clergy assume too prominent a role in managing the structures and activities of the institutional church. And second, we tend to view the institutional church as coextensive with the life of the people of God. The first confusion might be labeled "clericalism," or "proclericalism." The second might be labeled "ecclesiasticism."

We have already indicated some of the important areas of church life in which the clergy play a dominant role. But very few of these areas are such that they are the *sole* responsibility of clergy. Ministers and priests have special and unique functions in such areas as preaching and sacraments; but even here it is not necessary to view such matters as ones in which they alone are involved. The opening up of these areas to some degree of lay participation has been one of the healthy dimensions of liturgical reform in recent years. Other areas that have already been mentioned—visitation of the sick, counseling, youth work, and the like—are perhaps even more susceptible to lay involvement and direction.

"Ecclesiasticism"

Ecclesiasticism involves an overrating not only of the clergy but also of the institutional church itself. When this occurs, the dangers of clericalism are intensified; the clergy are then accorded a much too prominent place in an institution that is itself accorded a much too prominent place.

It is difficult to put the case against ecclesiasticism in such a manner that it will be acceptable to Christians from a variety of theological traditions. So I will begin by stating it in the terminology of my own Reformed tradition. Some Calvinists, particularly of the Dutch Reformed variety, are fond of making a distinction between "the church as an institution" and "the church as an organism." By the first term is meant the body of Christian believers as it is organized for very specific purposes, primarily worship (or, as some would put it, "cultic worship"). Included here would be the worshiping community that meets at a specific time and at a specific place, its organized patterns of interaction, and the larger network—a denomination or a "conference" or an association of congregations—of which it is a part.

The second term—"church as organism"—refers to the much larger community of Christians of which the institutional church is one segment, albeit an important one. This includes the Christian family, Christian educational institutions, Christian vocational groups, such as Christian business fellowships and other voluntary religious groups, as well as the many activities in which Christians are involved in the course of their everyday lives: labor, recreation, partying, buying and selling, sexual activity, study, music, drama, art, and so on. The church as an organism, in this sense, encompasses all the ways in which Christians seek, or ought to seek, to live out their lives as Christians in the world. Thus we might think of the first sense of "church" as referring to the church at worship (and related activities), while the second sense of "church" has to do with Christians functioning, whether communally or individually, as wives and husbands, workers and neighbors, quarterbacks and politicians, students and Red Cross volunteers.

Not all Christians will agree with this way of stating the case. Many Roman Catholics, for example, would be displeased about introducing two senses of "church" as described above. The differences ought not to be dismissed as merely terminological ones. To point out one implication, the Dutch Calvinists who employ this distinction between two senses of "church" establish "Christian schools" that are, as a matter of principle, independent of institutional-church control; such schools are viewed as a part of the organism-church, pursuing Christian goals in the area of education, but beyond the borders of the church as an institution. Roman Catholicism, again as a matter of principle, sponsors "parochial" schools, i.e., ecclesiastically controlled schools.

However, many Roman Catholics would be willing to make *something* like the distinction I have introduced. Even though the authority of the institutional church extends further for Roman Catholics than for most Protestants, Roman Catholicism countenances Christian organizations and activities that are for all practical purposes independent of ecclesiastical control. The "charismatic renewal" movement, for example, has even led to the development of "para-church" worshiping groups in which lay persons exercise spiritual authority, and even some clearly "magisterial" functions, apart from the direct supervision of the church.

The Laity in the World

In spite of the differences we might want to introduce, then, when stating the point in the terms and nuances of "official" theologies, there does seem to be an important distinction to be made somewhere in this neighborhood. The institutional church is not coextensive with the body of Christ; the full life of the people of God encompasses much more than what takes place in church buildings; the present reality of the kingdom of Jesus includes much more than what we ordinarily identify as the affairs of "the church." And this "more than the church" dimension of the Christian life is not a mere theological afterthought for most Christian laity. It has to do with the portion of reality in which we often find ourselves. When we talk about this area, we are dealing with the context in which most of the difficult and puzzling, and even painful, decisions arise for lay people. We are talking about what it is for us to be in "the world," that larger human community—with its institutions and structures—in which we are called to serve as ministers of the gospel of Jesus.

Lay people have not always viewed their calling to minister in the world with the seriousness required. Indeed, they have often avoided their calling in spite of noble efforts on the part of clergy and other church leaders to provide resources and encouragement for the worldly mission of the laity. In the final analysis, lay people must bear much of the blame for their own failures. And they must assume much of the responsibility for equipping themselves for ministry in the future. The clergy cannot do the laity's work for them, nor can the institutional church alone provide properly contextualized answers to the problems and dilemmas of the laity.

In recent years some clergy and church bureaucrats have engaged in what is perhaps an unprecedented process of self-examination, which has involved a struggling with very basic questions about the nature of their calling. The laity can do no less if they are to function in the world as agents of the reign of Jesus.

3

The People of God in the World

WE HAVE already referred many times to the "worldly" laity. There are some Christians who would find it strange that we could commend someone for being "worldly." For them, worldliness is a bad thing, to be avoided at all costs.

Christians who feel this way have some biblical support for their position. There is a kind of worldliness the Bible condemns. When the word *world* appears in English translations of the Bible, it can mean a number of different things. Sometimes it refers to the present sinful order that permeates the creation, and especially human society. The Apostle John told the early Christians that they ought not to "love the world or the things in the world" (1 John 2:15). Jesus himself is recorded as warning his disciples that since they are "not of the world" they should not be surprised if "the world hates you" (John 15:19). And in one of the most poignant asides in his epistles Paul tells us that his friend Demas had "deserted me and gone to Thessalonica," because he was "in love with this present world" (2 Tim. 4:10). In this sense to love the world is to be attached to those things that are, from the perspective of Christ's kingdom, transitory and illusory; it is to adopt the values of the sinful social order.

Another sense of "the world" in the Bible has neither a negative nor a positive connotation. It has to do with geography. For example, Jesus predicted that the "gospel of the kingdom will be preached throughout the whole world, as a testimony to all nations" (Matt. 24:14). Here "the world" is a physical expanse, the territory containing the peoples of the earth.

But a third sense does carry a positive meaning. In this sense of "world" it is proper for the Christian to *love* the world. Indeed, in this sense God himself is a lover of the world, as is made clear in that simplest of all biblical summaries of the gospel: "For God so loved the world that he gave his only Son, that whoever believes in him should not perish but have eternal life" (John 3:16). The Greek word here is *cosmos*, referring to the *created order*. This creation is presently distorted by sin and rebellion, but it is not unsalvageable. Thus, Jesus came "not to condemn the world, but that the world might be saved through him" (John 3:17). The creator God who judged his creation to be "very good" at its beginnings (Gen. 1:31) has reaffirmed its fundamental worth by sending his son to renew it.

Christians have obligations to the world in all three senses of the term. We are sent into the sinful order. As Jesus prayed to the Father on behalf of his disciples: "I do not pray that thou shouldst take them out of the world, but that thou shouldst keep them from the evil one" (John 17:15). Christians are called to penetrate the arena over which sin presently rules. This penetration in turn serves two purposes, corresponding to the two other senses of "world": we must bring the gospel to the world, in a territorial sense, going to the ends of the earth so that all may hear the good news; and we must identify with all that is good in the cosmos, the good creation.

The Gospel and Creation

In a very complex sense, then, the gospel is directed toward the world. This means that the Christian message extends beyond a mere concern for the individual; it has implications for the whole creation. The gospel is God's response to sin, and sin affects the whole of the world that God has made. The curse of sin is cosmic in scope. For one thing, the sinful rebellion of Adam and Eve has, according to Genesis 3, ramifications for the nonhuman natural order. Although this is a matter that is shrouded in some mystery, when Adam and Eve disobeyed God's commands a curse was introduced into the creation that apparently sent shock waves throughout the nonhuman realm: "cursed is the ground because of you . . . thorns and thistles it shall bring forth to you" (Gen. 3:17–18); and the Old Testament prophets view hostilities among the animals as a manifestation of sinfulness (see, e.g., Isa. 11:6–7).

But there is another sense in which the curse of sin affects more than the individual human beings: it also touches human institutions. Human greed, prejudice, selfishness, and pride—these attributes, which may well have their origins in the individual human heart, come to be woven into our institutional life, into the corporate patterns of human interaction. Institutions in turn perpetuate and reinforce these attributes in indivduals.

That this is so is clear from the phenomenon of racism. In the past, blacks in North America, South Africa, and other white-dominated societies were viewed as inferior human beings, even subhuman. Racist beliefs were consciously accepted and propagated by white people. These beliefs were translated into action. Blacks were enslaved or were assigned to the most menial tasks. They were deprived of basic human rights. They were made the butt of demeaning jokes and stories. These conscious practices in turn became corporate embodiments with a "life of their own." Racist attitudes were reflected in the legal system and in the labor market. The jokes and stories were passed on from generation to generation and came to be accepted as expressing obvious truths. The black community was systematically demoralized, constantly running up against stereotypes and prejudices.

It is no simple matter to change a situation of this sort. It is certainly not enough to say, as some Christians are fond of saying, that "changed hearts will change society." Racial prejudice may well have begun in individual human hearts, but it has now become institutionalized, codified. It is not enough for individual white people to say, "Now I will begin to treat them differently." Constitutions have to be rewritten; labor codes have to be changed; jokes and stories must be debunked; self-images need to be repaired; communities have to be rebuilt.

The transformation of institutional patterns is included in the biblical picture of redemption, as is the healing of nature. When the prophets envision the fulfillment of God's saving purposes, they portray a renewed creation: animals are at peace with one another and with human beings; the earth yields abundant produce; the weapons of war are exchanged for instruments of harvest; justice, righteousness, and peace are the rule of the day.

Witnesses for Redemption

Christians are called to be both witnesses to, and agents of, this full redemption. The institutional church is an important focal point for our involvement in this redemptive activity. For one thing, the church is the place—or one crucial place—where we reinforce our identity as redemptive witnesses and agents. God's goal of renewing his creation is one he pursues through an important strategy: the creation of a new people. This people, the community of those who accept God's offer of redemption, is the context in which he *begins* his renewing work.

And so Christians are called to *be* the community of God's people. They are called to realize in their communal life the "firstfruits" of redemption. The way in which we relate to each other as Christians, then, is a significant feature of our participation in the work of redemption. The way in which we conduct our ecclesiastical business, study, preach, pray, sing, organize for various tasks and activities— all of this is important to our identity as God's renewed people. And the institutional church is a crucial focal point for living out this identity.

But the existence of the institutional church is not an end in itself. The God of the Bible is not content with establishing a church. The church exists for some larger purpose. It is, as we have already indicated, a tactic in a larger plan. God's ultimate goal is the renewal of the creation; and the church exists as a central and important *means* for this renewal.

There are, of course, many difficult questions involved in deciding just how the church is to contribute to the renewal of the world. We will turn to these questions further on. But for the present it is important that we examine some of the basic elements of the life of the Christian community from a biblical point of view.

In the following pages we will examine some biblical themes at considerable length. In certain sectors of Protestantism, especially those with which I am most familiar, it is expected that an argument about some significant Christian concern will be backed up by an appeal to "what the Bible says." I believe that this expectation is both legitimate and praiseworthy.

Since the following discussion of biblical themes is the longest single portion of this book, a word of explanation may be necessary for some readers. It is my own conviction that a clear grasp of the calling of the laity can be attained only by a careful examination of the message of the Scriptures. This is not to say that we can find answers to difficult contemporary questions simply by citing biblical texts. There is much that we have to do by way of struggling to apply the biblical message to our own situation. But that struggle must be firmly rooted in an understanding of what the Bible says about the nature and calling of the people of God.

The struggle to get a clear idea about the biblical message is especially important with regard to our present topic. Lay people, we have been arguing, are called to be "worldly." They are required to bring Christian sensitivities to bear on their participation in the structures of the good creation. But *how* are they to relate to these structures? How, for example, ought Christians to view the authority patterns of the larger human community? Should Christians always obey the State? Should they try to "Christianize" the larger society by working for the establishment of laws that will guarantee "correct" behavior on the part of non-Christians? What happens when the demands of citizenship in the larger nation conflict with the demands of Christian conscience?

It is my conviction that the Bible does speak to questions of this sort. In both the Old and the New Testament the people of God received instructions as to how they were to act in situations similar to the ones addressed by these contemporary questions. Consequently, it seems very important to look at the ways in which these matters are treated by the biblical writers. The ultimate worth of this investigation will, of course, be decided by seeing whether it does, or does not, help us in understanding the shape of our present task as Christian lay people. Since I am convinced that this challenge will be met successfully in the following discussion, I invite the reader to bear with me—if need be, with patience.

A Charter for the People of God

It is no accident that many of the books and articles that discuss the laity from a biblical perspective contain some reference to 1 Peter 2. In this marvelous chapter the Apostle outlines the shape of the life of the Christian community as that community seeks to live obediently in the world. Verses 9 through 17 constitute a kind of "charter" for the corporate life of the New Testament community:

9 But you are a chosen race, a royal priesthood, a holy nation, God's own people, that you may declare the wonderful deeds of him who called you out of darkness into his marvelous light. 10 Once you were no people but

now you are God's people; once you had not received mercy but now you have received mercy.

11 Beloved, I beseech you as aliens and exiles to abstain from the passions of the flesh that wage war against your soul. 12 Maintain good conduct among the Gentiles, so that in case they speak against you as wrongdoers, they may see your good deeds and glorify God on the day of visitation.

13 Be subject for the Lord's sake to every human institution, whether it be to the emperor as supreme, 14 or to governors as sent by him to punish those who do wrong and to praise those who do right. 15 For it is God's will that by doing right you should put to silence the ignorance of foolish men. 16 Live as free men, yet without using your freedom as a pretext for evil; but live as servants of God. 17 Honor all men. Love the brotherhood. Fear God. Honor the emperor.

We shall examine this passage at some length, showing its connections, where that might be helpful, to other parts of the biblical message. This passage seems to divide conveniently into three sections. In verses 9 and 10 the Apostle establishes the continuity between Israel of the Old Testament and the New Testament Christian community; in verses 11 and 12 he singles out one stage of the history of Old Testament Israel as the appropriate context for viewing the calling of the New Testament church; then in verses 13 through 17 he lays down some general guidelines for the Christian community's involvement in the larger society within which it finds itself.

The Relationship between the Testaments

Let us examine the first section. The words of the Apostle here are a genuine stumbling block to many Christians who want to draw rigid lines between the Old and New Testaments. For example, some Christians have set up the contrast in this fashion: in the Old Testament, they say, God's redemptive dealings were with a nation or a people; but in the New Testament, there is a shift—God is now concerned primarily with individuals.

It is not to be denied that there is a development within the Bible in the direction of concern for the individual. There are parts of the Old Testament in which great emphasis is placed on group identity and group responsibility, to the degree that the worth and the responsibility of the individual seem to be ignored or downgraded. But this is not a matter on which we can simply draw a contrast between the Old and

New Testaments. Already in the Old Testament, there is a movement in the direction of individualization. Indeed, some commentators have referred to Jeremiah, for example, as an "individualist."

Of course, anyone reading through the Bible for the first time will be struck by the very special concern for individuals that appears in the ministry of Jesus. Here is individualizing love in its noblest form. Jesus stops in the midst of a crowd in response to a touch at the hem of his garment. He looks up into a tree and calls Zacchaeus by name. He tells a story about a shepherd who risks his life to find one lost sheep. This intense interest in individuals is not lost on the New Testament church.

But neither is the realization of the importance of peoplehood lost on the New Testament writers. Thus, Peter can write here to the New Testament community of Christians: "You are a chosen race, a royal priesthood, a holy nation, God's own people." The application of these images to the church establishes a direct and continuous relationship between Old Testament Israel and the believing community of the New Testament age.

Each of these images is applied to Israel in the Old Testament. The most obvious reference, which Peter undoubtedly has in mind here, is Exodus 19:6: "and you shall be to me a kingdom of priests and a holy nation." Similarly, Deuteronomy 7:6: "For you are a people holy to the Lord your God; the Lord your God has chosen you to be a people for his own possession, out of all the peoples that are on the face of the earth."

The primary purpose of the church, as Peter describes it here, is to "declare the wonderful deeds of him who called you out of darkness into his marvelous light." This, too, is an allusion to the calling of Israel. "The people who have walked in darkness have seen a great light" (Isa. 9:2); "and they shall declare my glory among the nations" (Isa. 66:19). Israel, too, went from being "no people" to being "my people"; "and I will say to Not my people, 'You are my people' " (Hos. 2:23).

New Meanings

On one level, then, the Apostle is simply drawing on a rich store of Old Testament imagery, applying titles and concepts that were once applied to the Jewish people of the covenant to the followers of Jesus.

But these images also take on new meanings in the New Testament context. Take the reference to the church as a "royal priesthood." The writer of Exodus does speak of Israel as a "kingdom of priests," but this idea does not "take" very well in the Old Testament. A specific priestly caste develops, with a special access to the holy places. The priests of the Old Testament serve in important respects as mediators between the ordinary people and God. The Exodus promise, then, serves as a kind of hint at something that never quite comes about in the Old Testament. The ordinary Israelite is not in any significant sense a "priest." He or she must rely on a special group of priestly mediators.

What is only vaguely hinted at in the Old Testament is now fully realized in Jesus Christ. Peter is aware of this and has already dealt with the theme in earlier verses. Because Jesus shed his "precious blood . . . like that of a lamb without blemish or spot" (1 Pet. 1:19), we can now "be a holy priesthood, to offer spiritual sacrifices acceptable to God through Jesus Christ" (1 Pet. 2:5). The priestly function, which was previously tied to a cultic office, is now attributed to the body of all believers. We have direct access to God through Christ. And the totality of our lives, our good deeds, will now be received by God as acceptable sacrifices to him.

The writer of the book of Revelation also uses a similar phrase to the one used here by Peter. His reference occurs in the context of a song that is sung before God's throne to the Lamb of God:

> Worthy art thou to take the scroll and to open its seals,
> for thou wast slain and by thy blood didst ransom men for God
> from every tribe and tongue and people and nation,
> and hast made them a kingdom and priests to our God,
> and they shall reign on earth.
>
> (Rev. 5:9–10)

This song rather explicitly points to some matters that are also implied in Peter's comments. The church may be a "chosen race," but it is a very special sort of "race." It is, in fact, a new kind of social entity whose very basis for existence is the miraculous work of redemption in Christ.

The church is a "race" formed out of the many tribes and tongues and peoples and nations of the earth. It is a new unity forged out of the brokenness of the human community. The confusion of tongues at the

Tower of Babel created a situation in which racial and ethnic plurality became a fact of life. Out of that situation God chose one specific ethnic people, Israel, and conferred his covenantal blessings on her as his very special possession. But the new "holy nation" that is now made possible by the blood of Jesus is not established on racial or ethnic foundations. Thus, our unity in Christ must be viewed as replacing the bonds that we may have previously experienced on the basis of "natural" racial, ethnic, or cultural ties. The gift of "tongues" at Pentecost has shattered the bonds that were established by the confusion of tongues at Babel.

Christian Nationhood

Of special interest for our present purposes is Peter's reference here to the church as a "holy nation." As this title applied to Old Testament Israel, it was, of course, literally correct. Israel was a nation. The term *nation* had a somewhat richer connotation in ancient times than it often has today. It certainly was more than a political term. To be a nation was to be a people with a common cultural, ethnic, and linguistic heritage. For Israel national identity was intimately related to religious identity as well.

But the term was not bereft of political meaning. To be a nation was to submit to political authority; it involved common allegiance to a political administration. In ancient Israel political authority was closely intertwined with other dimensions of life: educational, familial, religious, economic, aesthetic, legal, moral.

Israel was also a *holy* nation. She was a people who owed her existence to mighty deeds God had performed on her behalf: the call of Abram, the deliverance from Egypt, the travels through the wilderness, the entry into the promised land—each of these was sustained by miraculous interventions and divine leadings. Israel acknowledged her existence as a nation established through divine favor by structuring her political life "theocratically." *Theocracy* means "rule by God." This has to do with the basic pattern and understanding of political authority. In a theocracy authority and rule originate in the will of God—just as democratic authority resides in "the people" and aristocratic authority resides in a group of aristocrats.

Theocracy can take many shapes, as can democracy and aristocracy. And theocracy did manifest itself in many forms throughout the life of Israel. A "direct" theocracy would be a pattern of ruling whereby God revealed specific policies on a day-to-day basis, by announcing them directly to the citizenry. As a consistent pattern we do not find any examples of direct theocracy in the Old Testament (except perhaps in the Garden of Eden). Israel seems to have experienced a series of theocratic arrangements that were indirect or "mediatorial" in form. At each stage there seem to have been persons or groups who had special access to the will of God and who served as mediators between God and the masses of people.

At first God revealed his will to patriarchal leaders. Then there emerged certain wise men and women who had special access to the will of God. These gifted individuals came to have a certain quasi-official status as "judges." Later, human kings often had direct access to God: David and Solomon, for example. Even later, kings often had to turn to prophets and prophetesses to find out what God required.

At each point, nonetheless, the basic pattern is theocratic. God is the ruler of Israel. His word is what guides the life of the nation. These various arrangements—mediation on the part of wise persons, judges, kings, prophets, and prophetesses—are all means for discerning the will of God for the nation. This is not to say that Israel always *conformed* to the will of God. She often disobeyed and rebelled. She had wicked kings and followed the directions of false prophets. But these deviations were departures from her profession. Throughout her history she remained "officially" theocratic.

Israel was, then, a "holy nation," a God-ruled people, a theocracy. And this had a straightforward *political* meaning in the life of Israel. God was the highest political authority; his will was the ultimate appeal in political administration. Israel—at her best, at least—attempted to bring all her institutions and patterns of interaction into conformity with the will of God, her ultimate king.

Peter says that the church is also a "holy nation." What shall we make of this? The underlying purpose here is to point to similarities between Israel and the church. But in what sense is the church also a "nation"?

At the very least the Apostle seems to be using this term to point to the closely knit, cohesive network of relations we take upon ourselves when we become Christians. The bond that exists among members of the New Testament community of Christians ought to be at least as strong as that which held among the people of Israel. The sense of loyalty that resulted from being a Jew in the Old Testament days must be matched by those who have been incorporated into the new community of Christ followers.

But the application of this term to the church goes beyond a mere metaphorical reference to the cohesiveness of the Christian community. It also says something about how the gospel reorders our previous loyalties and commitments. We must remember that Peter was writing to citizens of the Roman Empire. These Christians lived in a cultural environment in which many claims were made on their loyalties. Not the least of these claims was that of the Roman state itself. Rome often attempted to elicit from its citizens a loyalty that was virtually "religious" in nature.

Many writers have pointed out that the early Christian confession "Jesus is Lord" was, in the context of the Roman Empire, a profoundly political statement. The Roman Caesars at times attempted to establish themselves as "lords," as sovereign rulers over all dimensions of life. They often demanded a loyalty from their citizens that had an ultimacy about it. When Christians confessed, then, that Jesus is Lord, they were also issuing a denial: "and Caesar is *not* Lord."

In that environment the insistence that the church is a "nation" is one that also has profound political implications. It is a way of saying that no other institution or regime can claim our absolute loyalties. If the church is a holy nation of which we are citizens, we must be very careful about what we offer to the other "nations" in which we find ourselves. Our Christian citizenship must always be foremost in our minds; it must be our point of reference when the claims of other "citizenships" are thrust upon us.

The reference to the church as a "nation" also speaks to the issue of authority patterns in the Christian community. The church, like Israel, is a *theocratic* community. Christians are members of that community over which Jesus reigns as King. The church—and I refer here to the "church" in the broadest sense, as including, but going beyond, the institutional church—exists under the rule of Jesus. It is not brought into existence by human beings; if we were left to our own designs, we would still be "no people." It exists to serve the will of

him who allows no rivals when it comes to claiming our ultimate
loyalties.

The Quest for Identity

These words of the Apostle Peter, with which he establishes the
lines of continuity between the Old and New Testaments, speak with
a kind of direct clarity to our own age. We need only think of the
various quests for "peoplehood" that have occurred in this century
and the various ways in which human beings have sought an identity
as a "chosen race" or a "holy nation": the boastful claims on behalf
of a German or Afrikaner *volk;* the prideful appeals to the alleged
purity of race and Klan in North America; the vain quests for ideal
"communities," as manifested in the hippie commune or the "encounter session"; the desperate search for salvation by submission to
a variety of codes and authority figures, whether the quest ends in the
donning of a "Hell's Angels" jacket, or in membership in a Manson-
type "family," or in citizenship in a Jonestown, or in residing in a
"swinging singles" condominium.

The Bible speaks to these quests for "community" and "racial
purity" and "self-realization." In the midst of the confusing array of
contemporary quests for new "identities" the Apostle's pronounce-
ment has a prophetic ring: "But you are a chosen race, a royal
priesthood, a holy nation, God's own people." The quest for peoplehood is legitimate from a biblical perspective. But that quest will not
be properly realized under the sign of the swastika or under the
banner of racism. True priesthood will not be found by means of
hallucinogenic experiments or macho rites of initiation. Proper
nationhood will not be discovered by patriotic hysteria or militaristic
rantings.

Peoplehood can be discovered only at the cross. We become members of a chosen race only by being received into that multiracial
community whose right to exist was purchased by the Lamb without
blemish. Citizenship in a holy nation comes about only by submission
to the rule of Jesus.

Some Christians have shied away in recent years from using the
phrase "the people of God." They fear that these words are too easily
misunderstood. Their underlying concern is a legitimate one. But we

must not allow that variety of quests for false peoplehood to blunt the biblical call to true peoplehood.

In this regard it is especially important that we not let our status as "the people of God" be the occasion for pride. When Christians boast of their special status as a chosen people, it is precisely at that point that they run the risk of *losing* that status. We are called to peoplehood, not to point to ourselves, but to show forth the wonderful deeds of him who called us out of darkness. To be God's priestly people is to give our lives to the service of the needy and oppressed. To be a holy nation is to aid in delivering prisoners from their captivity. To be a chosen race is to refuse to claim any "purity" except the purity of Jesus' blood.

Old Testament Stages

We must turn to the second section of our passage, verses 11 and 12. In the previous verses Peter had referred to the church as, among other things, a holy nation. We have already indicated that this serves to establish a similarity between the Christian community and Israel of the Old Testament. Now in this second section the Apostle elaborates further on the relationship between Israel and the church: "Beloved, I beseech you as aliens and exiles . . . " (1 Pet. 2:11).

Old Testament Israel went through a number of different stages in its mode of social organization. My meaning here can be clarified by looking briefly at five of the most dominant patterns. We can begin with the captivity in Egypt. Here Israel was a slave people, held in bondage in a land not considered to be its own. This period ends with the Exodus from Egypt. As a result of God's miraculous intervention on their behalf the Israelites are released from slavery, and they embark on a second pattern of social organization: that of a nomadic people, wandering in the wilderness in search of a homeland that has been promised to them by God.

The third period begins on their coming into possession of the land of Canaan. Here they settle into a "landed theocracy." This pattern, as we have already indicated, proceeds through various adjustments—tribal patriarchy, rule by judges, the anointing of human kings—but it is characterized throughout by a mode of existence whereby Israel is self-ruled in a land that is her own. (For the sake of simplicity here, I am ignoring the distinction between the two kingdoms, Israel and Judah.)

Then Israel is overrun by an enemy force, and significant portions of her people are carried off to other places by her captors. This is the period of exile or dispersion. Finally, many of the exiles return to the homeland, but the land is soon invaded again. In the intertestamental period, and at the time of the gospel accounts, then, we have Israel (at least many Israelites) in the homeland again, but living under an occupying force.

Contemporary Applications

We can give these stages one-word labels: slavery, wandering, homeland, exile, and occupation. It is interesting to note that images from each of these periods enter into the languages of Christian groups today. The thesis here might be put this way: Christians tend to identify themselves with Israel of the Old Testament; in doing so, a Christian group will choose images associated with one or more of the stages we have listed; the stage or stages alluded to tell us something about the character or self-understanding of the group in question.

For example, the black American slave in previous centuries often identified closely with Israel's enslavement in Egypt: "Let my people go." This was a natural pattern of identification, since it is quite proper for Christian people to draw parallels between their own experience and that of Israel. The black slaves never, as far as I can tell, identified with Israel when she possessed her own land and maintained her own "landed" institutions. And understandably so: black people, especially poor blacks, in North America have seldom felt as if they did "possess" a land.

We also find the slaves, and their contemporary descendants, drawing on images of nomadic wandering and exile. They have a collective memory of having been wrenched away from their homeland and forcibly thrust into a strange land. In black spirituals the biblical heroes referred to are primarily those of the Exodus and exile: Moses and Daniel figure prominently.

Images of nomadic wandering have been self-consciously appropriated by the Mennonites and others associated with the radical Anabaptist tradition. Not long ago I was a guest lecturer on a Mennonite college campus. One morning I paid a visit to the historical collection on that campus, and the resident archivist gave me a brief account of this particular Mennonite group. Their origins date back to seventeenth-century Netherlands, but after severe persecution there they moved to Prussia. Later they migrated to Russia, and then finally they came to the southwestern part of the United States. He showed me church records in which entries were written at each location where the group had lived. The curious thing was that when these Mennonites lived in Prussia, their records were written in the Dutch language; while in Russia, they used the German language.

I asked the obvious question: "Isn't it rather strange that they refused to use the language of the land in which they were living? Why did they always write in the language of the place where they had just previously lived?" The archivist smiled and said: "We Mennonites like to think of ourselves as strangers in the land. We never want to feel at home. So we find ways of expressing our sense of being exiled!" This same sense of exile has been expressed in the songs and hymns of North American evangelicalism and fundamentalism: "This world is not my home, I'm just a-passing through," "I've got a mansion over the hilltop," "Guide me, O thou great Jehovah, Pilgrim through this barren land."

The North American Puritans provide us with a good example of a group that switched from the images of one stage to those of another. When the Puritans first came to New England, they thought of themselves as Israel wandering in the wilderness in search of the promised land. (The title of Perry Miller's classic discussion of Puritanism, *Errand into the Wilderness,* illustrates this theme. For an excellent study of this image in Puritanism, see Robert Bellah's *The Broken Covenant.*) But after they settled into the land, they came to think of themselves as having established "Jerusalem" or "Zion." The Puritan settlements were thought of as constituting "a city set upon a hill" and a "light to the nations." The same transition from a wandering people to a "Zion" people can be observed in the history of the Afrikaner people of South Africa (a matter discussed in a helpful manner by Willem de Klerk in his *Puritans in Africa*).

As we have already seen, the images of exile or dispersion tend to become merged with those of wandering in the wilderness and slavery. The fifth stage, that of living in one's own land under an occupying force, shows up when the conviction is expressed that one is living in God's creation but that the creation is presently in the grip of Satan and his legions. The imagery of occupation is also utilized by those Christians who live in lands that are controlled by what they view to be alien forces, as was the case, for example, with people who lived under Nazi occupation and still is with black South Africans, and Christians in Communist countries.

Actually, for our general purposes four of these stages can be grouped together. Slavery, wandering, exile, and occupation are alike in the sense that in each case Israel was alienated from her present social setting—she was not "at home." The homeland or "Zion" stage was one in which she viewed matters as "normal"; she was "at home" in the land.

The Exile Theme

This Old Testament background is necessary to understand Peter's way of addressing the church in this passage: "Beloved, I beseech you as aliens and exiles." This is the second time he uses the language of exile in this epistle. The opening salutation of the epistle employs the same theme: "Peter, an apostle of Jesus Christ, to the exiles of the dispersion in Pontus, Galatia, Cappadocia, Asia, and Bithynia . . ." (1 Pet. 1:1).

Why does Peter address the New Testament church as a community of "aliens and exiles"? It is not sufficient to answer this question by insisting that Peter was writing exclusively, or even primarily, to Jewish Christians—who might then be thought of as literally being members of the dispersed Israel. Nor is it the case that all Peter's readers, including his Gentile readers, were in some sense "exiled" from the land of their proper earthly citizenship.

Rather, Peter here seems to be making a *theological* point. He is indicating how we are to understand the *status* of the church in the present age. He is saying that as we try to get clear about how we as Christians are related to the surrounding societies in whose contexts we live, we ought to think of ourselves as dispersed or exiled Israel.

It is generally agreed by commentators that this is also how we should understand the opening words of the Epistle of James, which utilizes the same theme as Peter's salutation: "James, a servant of God and of the Lord Jesus Christ, to the twelve tribes in the dispersion" (James 1:1). Here, too, James is addressing an audience that is not exclusively Hebrew and that contains persons who are not in some other sense literally exiled from the land of their earthly citizenship. Indeed, it is because of these opening words that the Epistle of James is often described as one of the "catholic" epistles. Its address to "the twelve tribes in the dispersion" is taken to be a statement that the epistle is not addressed to a set of local problems but is meant for Christians living under a variety of different conditions.

This emphasis on the Christian community as a community in exile, alienated from the social status quo, is a consistent theme throughout the New Testament. Jesus viewed his own ministry in terms of homelessness: "Foxes have holes, and birds of the air have nests; but the Son of man has nowhere to lay his head" (Matt. 8:20). And he instructed his disciples to "shake off the dust from your feet" as they encountered hostility in their travels (Matt. 10:14).

In Hebrews 11, in which numerous parallels are drawn between Old Testament heroes and heroines, it is striking that no parallel is drawn between the condition of the church and the "Zion" situation of the Old Testament. Rather, the examples are consistently spelled out in terms of social alienation. These Old Testament saints "sojourned in the land of promise, as in a foreign land"; they "looked forward to the city which has foundations, whose builder and maker is God"; they "all died in faith, not having received what was promised, but having seen it and greeted it from afar, and having acknowledged that they were strangers and exiles on the earth. . . . they desire a better country, that is, a heavenly one. Therefore God . . . has prepared for them a city" (Heb. 11:9, 13, 16).

We ought to note that at least one passage in the Epistles seems, at first glance, to be a counterexample to our claim that the New Testament consistently views the Christian community as "strangers in the land." Ephesians 2:19 seems to sound a different note: "So then you are no longer strangers and sojourners, but you are fellow citizens with the saints and members of the household of God." But this refers to a different matter from the one we are discussing. The Apostle is speaking here to "Gentiles in the flesh" who were once "alienated from the commonwealth of Israel, and strangers to the covenants of promise" (Eph. 2:11–12). Through Christ these Gentiles have now been made heirs to the promises that were once offered to Israel. They are now citizens of the "new Israel," the church.

But Peter (as well as James and the writer to the Hebrews) is discussing the present status of this new commonwealth, to which both Jew and Gentile are now called in Christ. And he is suggesting that this people must now view their condition as being like that of Israel in exile.

Primary Citizenship

When the Israelites of the Old Testament were dispersed and exiled, they did not lose their citizenship in Israel. Even when they settled into the country in which they were exiled, they retained their Israelite identity. In such a situation they had dual citizenship, and it was never to be forgotten that their primary allegiance was to the commonwealth of Israel, even when that commonwealth did not retain a centralized government.

So it is with the church. Christians are first and foremost Christians, citizens of the theocratic commonwealth over which Jesus reigns as King. Even when they are in some sense "settled into" Canada, or the United States, or England, or Uganda, or South Korea, they are to view their specific relationships to the specific nation in question as similar to that of the Jew to Babylon. Furthermore, Christians look forward to a time when their exile will be ended, when the dispersed citizens of the holy commonwealth will be gathered from the ends of the earth. "They desire a better country, that is, a heavenly one. Therefore God . . . has prepared for them a city."

We should not ignore the fact here that some Christians will be less comfortable with this emphasis on "exile" than others will be. I doubt that I will be able to alleviate their discomfort completely here. It is simply a fact that the New Testament writers regularly refer to the Christian community as being in "exile." Of course, we must acknowledge an element of metaphor in this way of referring to the situation of Christians, although I am less inclined than others to make too much of the metaphorical element. The important point being stressed by the "exile" language, however, is the need for the Christian community to view its ultimate loyalties as being directed toward God's kingdom, against which all other loyalties and commitments must be measured. Christians must view themselves as not being completely "at home" in the present order. For those who are uncomfortable with the "exile" theme, the idea of "pilgrimage" may be preferable. Those persons may substitute "pilgrimage" wherever I use the term *exile*.

The further instructions given by Peter to the church, in both this second section and the third, are given as guidance to the church in its exile situation. "I beseech you as aliens and exiles to abstain from the passions of the flesh that wage war against your soul" (1 Pet. 2:11). We must not interpret "the flesh" here too narrowly. When we hear about "the flesh," we are inclined to think of our *bodies;* but that would be to miss Peter's point here.

When the Bible talks about "the flesh," it sometimes refers to human bodies, our physical functions and attributes—but not always. Often the biblical writers use the word *flesh* to refer to a way of thinking and living. Here the meaning is very close to one of the senses of "the world," as we discussed that topic earlier. To be of "the flesh" can be to pattern our thinking and living after the sinful order of things. It is to have a sinful *orientation*. Of course, one way to be "fleshly" in this sense is to overindulge our bodies: to be gluttons, or to engage in thoughts and actions that are sexually promiscuous. But there are other ways of being "fleshly."

Paul, in Galatians 5:19–21, includes in a list of the "works of the flesh" such items as "idolatry," "jealousy," "anger," and "party spirit." This points to a broad range of things that can be "fleshly": people can be "fleshly" by thinking too highly of their own mathematical abilities, or by placing their ultimate trust in a nation or a lodge, or by getting angry over a minor point of doctrine. We can be "fleshly" over highly intellectual or even "spiritual" matters.

There is good reason to interpret Peter's reference here in equally broad terms. The "passions of the flesh" are forces that "war against your soul." Elsewhere in this epistle Peter speaks of "the salvation of your souls" (1 Pet. 1:9), "having purified your souls by your obedience to the truth for a sincere love of the brethren" (1 Pet. 1:22), "the Shepherd and Guardian of your souls" (1 Pet. 2:25), and those who "entrust their souls to a faithful creator" (1 Pet. 4:19). The "passions of the flesh," then, come from those forces that attack the soul in these respects: they threaten our salvation, tempt us away from the truth, and separate us from our Shepherd, our faithful creator.

Good Conduct

The specific term of contrast to "fleshly" behavior Peter uses here is that of "good conduct": "Maintain good conduct among the Gentiles . . ." (1 Pet. 2:12). This term, *good conduct,* and its equivalents play a crucial role in this passage: "good conduct," "good deeds"; verse 14: "do right"; verse 15: "doing right."

The idea of "good conduct" also shows up in other passages in the apostolic letters that speak directly to the relationship of the Christian community to the institutions of the larger societies in which they find themselves. (As an oversimplification, we could call these "Church and State" passages.) They are: Romans 13:1–7; 1 Timothy 2:1–4; Titus 3:1–8; and our present passage 1 Peter 2:9–17. Similar ideas and phrases appear in all these passages (which has led some scholars to suggest that each of these passages borrows from a fifth document circulating in the churches).

The "good conduct" idea shows up in each: Romans 13:3: "For rulers are not a terror to good conduct. . . Then do what is good"; 1 Timothy 2:2–3: ". . . that we may lead a quiet and peaceable life, godly and respectful in every way. This is good . . ."; Titus 3:8 ". . . that those who have believed in God may be careful to apply themselves to good deeds; these are excellent and profitable to men."

To get a better idea of what the *substance* of these good deeds must be, we must wait to look at the third section of this passage in 1 Peter 2. But we can note here that when Israel in the Old Testament was carried off to Babylon, she was also instructed to perform good deeds. Not in these same words, of course; but the notion of performing good works was central to the instructions she received in her exile.

The most prominent passage in this regard is the set of instructions given to the exiled people in Jeremiah 29:1, 4–9:

> These are the words of the letter which Jeremiah the prophet sent from Jerusalem to the elders of the exiles, and to the priests, the prophets, and all the people, whom Nebuchadnezzar had taken into exile from Jerusalem to Babylon. . . . "Thus says the Lord of hosts, the God of Israel, to all the exiles whom I have sent into exile from Jerusalem to Babylon: Build houses and live in them; plant gardens and eat their

produce. Take wives and have sons and daughters; take wives for your sons, and give your daughters in marriage, that they may bear sons and daughters; multiply there, do not decrease. But seek the welfare of the city where I have sent you into exile, and pray to the Lord on its behalf, for in its welfare you will find your welfare. For thus says the Lord of Hosts, the God of Israel: Do not let your prophets and your diviners who are among you deceive you, and do not listen to the dreams which they dream, for it is a lie which they are prophesying to you in my name; I did not send them, says the Lord."

The Israelites are instructed here to take their citizenship in Babylon seriously. They are to plant gardens, gain their livelihood, and raise their families there. And they are actively to seek the welfare of the city and also pray on its behalf to the Lord. But at the same time they are not to be misled by false prophets, or to engage in superstitious practices. One parallel to these instructions in the New Testament is in the passage from 1 Timothy 2:1–2 already mentioned. There the Christian community is advised to offer "supplications, prayers, intercessions, and thanksgivings . . . for kings and all who are in high positions" and to "lead a quiet and peaceable life, godly and respectful in every way."

The Christian community, then, must also pray to the Lord on behalf of the city in which it dwells. And it must perform "good deeds"—a parallel to Jeremiah's "seek the welfare of the city." The "quiet and peaceable," "godly and respectful" life that is mentioned in the Timothy passage must not be viewed in the passive, in terms of "live and let live." Our godliness is to be manifested in our active good works, directed toward the welfare of the city.

But in this second section Peter quickly adds a comment that serves to warn against performing only those "good deeds" that will preserve the status quo or win the favor of all our neighbors: "so that in case they speak against you as wrongdoers, they may see your good deeds and glorify God on the day of visitation (1 Pet. 2:12). We must not merely *please* the "Gentiles" in whose midst we live. Indeed, they may well look at our "good deeds" and accuse us of being "wrongdoers." The kinds of good works we ought to perform are not deeds that will be immediately recognized for their merits; rather, they are deeds that will be *shown* to be good works on "the day of visitation."

The Final Accounting

Some commentators have suggested that "the day of visitation" refers to a periodic visit on the part of judges who are sent from Rome to hear local cases that have piled up over a given time span. Indeed, Peter refers to this institution in the next section: "to the emperor as supreme, or to governors as sent by him to punish those who do wrong and to praise those who do right" (1 Pet. 2:13–14). If this is the correct interpretation, Peter is telling the Christian community to perform those deeds that will stand up under the scrutiny of a circuit judge, even though they may be temporarily condemned by unbelieving neighbors.

What seems more likely is that Peter is referring to the day of the Lord's visitation—to the final accounting that will come in the Last Judgment. This interpretation gains credence from the fact that the idea of a final accounting is a common theme in this epistle: "so that the genuineness of your faith . . . may redound to praise and glory and honor at the revelation of Jesus Christ" (1:7); "set your hope fully upon the grace that is coming to you at the revelation of Jesus Christ" (1:13); "they will give account to him who is ready to judge the living and the dead" (4:5). Furthermore, the phrase "day of visitation" seems to be an Old Testament phrase, or a near equivalent to one, that does refer to a divine visitation. Isaiah asks, "What will you do on the day of punishment . . .?"—or as the King James Version translates it, "What will ye do in the day of visitation?" (Isa. 10:3). The more common Old Testament phrase "the time (or year) of punishment (or visitation)" appears at least nine times in the Old Testament and always includes an element of accounting before God.

But it doesn't really matter how we understand this particular phrase, since the crucial part of Peter's qualification here is that people will someday see our "good deeds and *glorify God* on the day of visitation." Whether the judge in question is human or divine, the crucial concern has to do with whether our deeds contribute to the glory of God. Needless to say, the phraseology Peter uses here is so close to that of the Lord Jesus himself that it is difficult to believe that Jesus' words are not consciously before Peter's mind: "Let your light so shine before men, that they may see your good works and give glory to your Father who is in heaven" (Matt. 5:16).

Specific Instructions

We turn now to the third section of this passage. Peter here turns to a set of more specific instructions for the believing community. The instructions are not so specific that they provide unambiguous guidance for every situation they bear on. Rather, they express some guidelines for the Christian community's interaction with the patterns of authority in the larger societies in which it lives. These instructions stipulate certain basic attitudes, and they suggest certain priorities.

The section begins with: "Be subject for the Lord's sake to every human institution" (1 Pet. 2:13). The issue being raised by this injunction is crucial for the self-understanding of the people of God, and especially for the way in which lay people understand their involvement in the structures in which they carry on their activities. Needless to say, there are matters of great importance at stake here. To ignore the New Testament calls to submission to human authority, even "secular" authority, is to miss a rather consistent theme of the apostolic writings. But to appeal glibly to these calls to "subjection" puts us in a situation where we run the risk of disobedience to the gospel.

This is an area of Christian thought and practice in which Christians have often proceeded with very little biblical or theological discipline. Most often we have formed attitudes on the appropriate patterns of submission to institutional authority with virtually no attention to biblical guidelines. We have followed the mood of the times, whether "conservative," "liberal," or "radical." Even where the Bible has been explicitly appealed to, this has often been characterized by a "proof-texting" or sloganeering mentality. Seldom have our attitudes been shaped by biblical study and theological reflection.

In recent years I have had numerous occasions to discuss Christian political attitudes with student groups on many college campuses, adult education classes in local churches, and in a variety of other contexts. From this sampling (admittedly limited) of very basic views held by Christians with regard to political authority, I have gained the clear impression that there are three "proof texts" regularly cited in support of a decidedly "passive" attitude toward the political status quo.

Rendering unto Caesar

The first of these proof texts is Jesus' response to those who asked him about the propriety of paying taxes to the Roman government: "Render to Caesar the things that are Caesar's, and to God the things that are God's." This comment has been used to support all sorts of patterns of acquiescence to the political status quo. Those who cite it regularly do so with the conviction that it provides a simple solution to some political dilemma: "Hasn't the government made it clear that it wants us to do so and so? And did not Jesus tell us to render to Caesar what belongs to him? Well, then, what is the argument all about? Isn't it clear what we are to do?"

This comment by Jesus is recorded by three of the gospel writers: Matthew 22:21; Mark 12:17; and Luke 20:25. Each writer places the comment in a context in which Jesus' opponents are trying to trip him up by forcing him to answer questions in a manner that will get him into trouble with some group that will then have the power to bring public accusations against him. For example, in the Luke account this comment occurs in the second of three confrontations with Jesus' antagonists, all recorded in chapter 20. First, they ask him about the source of his own authority. If he says that his authority comes from God, he will be accused of blasphemy; if he says that it is of human origin, he will undercut his ministry.

But instead of answering directly, Jesus fires a question back at his interlocutors: "Was the baptism of John from heaven or from men?" (Luke 20:4). His opponents immediately realize the dilemma in which he has placed them:

> And they discussed it with one another, saying, "If we say, 'From heaven,' he will say, 'Why did you not believe him?' But if we say, 'From men,' all the people will stone us; for they are convinced that John was a prophet." So they answered that they did not know whence it was. And Jesus said to them, "Neither will I tell you by what authority I do these things."
>
> (Luke 20:5–8)

Jesus doesn't give an unambiguous answer to their question. Nor does he in the third confrontation, where the Sadducees ask him about a woman who has seven successive marriages to seven brothers: "In the resurrection, therefore, whose wife will the woman be?" (Luke 20:33). Jesus refuses to answer the question, stating that resurrected persons "neither marry nor are given in marriage" (Luke 20:35)—an observation whose meaning is not exactly crystal clear.

The injunction to "render unto Caesar" must be understood in its context, as it is placed between these two other confrontations. (The other accounts of this comment place it in a similar context: Matthew says that the Pharisees were trying "to entangle him in his talk" [22:15]; and Mark has them trying to "entrap" him [12:13]. As Father Richard Cassidy puts it in his helpful discussion of this series of confrontations, there is "a feature common to all three of Jesus' replies: Jesus does not give a direct answer to the question originally addressed to him" [Richard J. Cassidy, *Jesus, Politics, and Society*, page 53]).

Jesus' comments on the political question, and many of his other sayings, must be viewed in relationship to four groups whose views figure into the political situation of his day. For purposes of a brief characterization the situation can be seen in the following way. On the "radical right" were the tax collectors, who were in the employ of the Roman government and who were closely aligned with its interests; on the "moderate right" were the Sadducees, whose theology permitted considerable accommodation to the Roman occupation. The Pharisee party was on the "moderate left"; they stressed conformity to the Jewish law and viewed theocracy as the ideal framework—thus their accommodation to Roman rule was at best an uneasy one. The Zealots, on the "radical left," were committed to the violent overthrow of the occupying force.

In this political situation the question of paying tribute to Caesar was a politically potent one. If Jesus approved of paying taxes to the Roman state, he would be giving ammunition to his opponents on the left. If he voiced objections to paying, he could be sure that his antagonists on the right would use this against him. The fact is that his answer gave comfort to neither side; they could not understand his meaning. We ought to pay Caesar, he said, what Caesar rightfully has coming to him; but we must surely not give him what belongs to God. This left all his opponents puzzled; for the question Jesus left open was, "what *does* rightfully belong to Caesar?" Did he really mean to say that whatever Caesar affixes his seal to thereby belongs to him? Can Caesar claim just *anything* he wants merely by decreeing that it belongs to him?

Jesus' answer here—by itself—is no more helpful to us than it was to his contemporaries. Indeed, it is far more interesting to the church for what it shows about the personality of Jesus, his cleverness, and his sense of humor than for its substance as a piece of political guidance. On this latter score, the most that it tells us is that we ought to mark out the boundaries of what belongs to Caesar and what belongs to God—boundaries that, because of the fact that everything ultimately belongs to God, will be difficult to ascertain. But it tells us nothing about where those boundaries are. To deal with that question we must reflect theologically on the full scope of the biblical message as it bears on the domain of politics.

Jesus' Kingship

The second proof text is Jesus' comment to Pilate: "My kingship is not of this world" (John 18:36). Many Christians use this remark by Jesus as a kind of cliché to defend the notion that his mission was a "spiritual" one. If Jesus had been interested in political confrontation, they say, he had a perfect opportunity when he stood before Pilate. But he avoided the confrontation.

What this line of argument ignores is the fact that Jesus was only *postponing* his confrontation with Pilate. Matthew reports that after the crucifixion Pilate ordered a guard of soldiers to make the tomb "as secure as you can" (Matt. 27:65). The tomb was then sealed and a guard was set. But this was to no avail, as we find out a few verses later: "And behold, there was a great earthquake; for an angel of the Lord descended from heaven and came and rolled back the stone" (Matt. 28:2).

The resurrection of Jesus was an illegal act, a defiance of Pilate's authority. It was, in an important sense, the first Christian act of civil disobedience. For on Easter morning the kingdom of Jesus and the kingdom of Pilate clashed. An angelic offensive was initiated against Pilate's squadron. Whatever Jesus meant, then, when he told Pilate that he—Jesus—represented a different sort of kingship, on Easter morning it became obvious that Pilate had no authority to cancel the resurrection.

An important test for interpreting the words of Jesus, and the words of the Apostles themselves, is to be applied by asking what the actual shape of these teachings was in the practice of the early church. In the Book of Acts the early Christians regularly came into conflict with civil authorities. In many places the preaching of the gospel was considered to be a threatening matter, and over and over local authorities attempted to curb or silence the witness of the Apostles. If the most conservative, "passive" interpretations of the teachings of Jesus were correct, we would expect the Apostles to acquiesce to the will of those who attempted to ban their activities. We would expect reasoning of this sort: "Do kings and others in high positions require us to cease our preaching? Well, then, we must cease, for we are to render to Caesar that which is Caesar's. . . ." "Haven't we been jailed for violating regulations laid down by duly constituted authorities? Well, then, we must remain where we are, for the kingdom which we serve is not of this world." "Is that an angel opening the door of our cell? Go away, please, and leave us be! We are to be subject to every human institution."

But, of course, this is not the way they reasoned. Instead, they boldly confronted local authorities with the proclamation: "We must obey God rather than men" (Acts 5:29). Like Mary and Joseph before them, they fled from the evil designs of politicians. And, following the example of Easter morning, they welcomed angels sent to break the seals of their prisons.

The Role of Government

The third proof text is, in fact, a phrase from the opening verse of Romans 13. Most often it is quoted from the King James version: "the powers that be are ordained of God." In this passage the Apostle Paul does portray the role of government in a very favorable light:

> Let every person be subject to the governing authorities. For there is no authority except from God, and those that exist have been instituted by God. Therefore he who resists the authorities resists what God has appointed, and those who resist will incur judgment. For rulers are not a terror to good conduct, but to bad. Would you have no fear of him who is in authority? Then do what is good, and you will receive his approval, for he is God's servant for your good. But if you do wrong, be afraid, for he does not bear the sword in vain; he is the servant of God to execute his wrath on the wrongdoer.   (Rom. 13:1–4)

This is a difficult passage to understand, and its interpretation has been much debated in the history of the church. We will not go into the many complexities here. The main point to be insisted on for our present purposes is this: it would be wrong to build a whole theology of the state on an interpretation of this passage in isolation from the rest of the biblical message. To say this is to recognize that, taken by itself, this passage says some things that suggest a "passive" posture on the part of the Christian community as it relates to civil government; God has instituted government; it serves his purposes; so to obey the government is to perform "good works" in the sight of God.

My own way of understanding this passage follows what is sometimes called the "normative" interpretation. In this view what the Apostle is doing here is describing the role of a *properly functioning* government. He is telling us that government has a proper place and role in human society and that this involves rewarding those who do good and punishing those who are wrongdoers. In such an ideal situation, then, we have nothing to fear from government if we concentrate on the performance of good works.

But even if some Christians may have reasons for rejecting some element of that interpretation, this much seems clear: it is impossible to take this passage as committing us to the view that we ought always to obey each and every dictate of any government that happens to be in power over us. This is impossible for at least three reasons. First, there is the overwhelming evidence from the actual practice of the Christian church from its earliest days. Following the Old Testament examples of Daniel, the young men who were sent to the fiery furnace, and others, the church has always maintained that at the very least no government has the right to limit the church's pursuit of what it understands to be the true worship of God. The Apostles themselves bear witness to this conviction, as do the Christians who worshiped (illegally) in the catacombs and tens of thousands of martyrs who faced ridicule, hungry lions, the stake, and the sword rather than to submit to idolatry, defilement of worship, or the dishonoring of the name of their Lord.

Second, it is impossible to hold such a view in the light of the general biblical testimony, however we interpret these particular words in Romans 13. Some writers have stressed in recent years that we must balance Romans 13 with Revelation 13. This latter passage describes a government that becomes like a beast, uttering blasphemies against God; there the saints of God refuse the domination of the beast—and rightly so. The biblical testimony seems clear: Christians ought not to obey governments that are committed to blasphemous attempts to thwart the saving purposes of God.

Third, the evidence of this passage in Romans 13 itself, and its immediate context, militates against such a view. It seems obvious that, when the Apostle tells us, in this passage, to perform "good works," this has a meaning that is independent of mere obedience to governmental dictates. It is not human authority that decides what is to count as "good works"—that is to be decided by consulting the will of God. It is impossible to read the verses immediately preceding and immediately following this passage (see Rom. 12:9–21 and 13:8–14) without becoming aware of the fact that the writer has very specific ideas as to what constitutes the life of "good works" for the Christian community. And there can be no doubt what our choice must be when a specific government attempts to ban or restrict—as has happened so often—the performance of these works.

Subjection

As we return to the third section of our passage in 1 Peter 2, we can note an obvious parallel between its context and that of Romans 13. Here, too, is the call to "be subject" to authorities whose task is understood in terms of the punishing of wrongdoers and the rewarding of "those who do right" (1 Pet. 2:14).

The idea of "subjection" here is one that we encounter over and over again in the apostolic writings. It is applied to various relations: wives are to be subject to their husbands; husbands and wives, to one another; children, to parents; slaves, to their masters; church members, to the leaders of the churches; and citizens, to rulers. A word study of the closely related Greek verbs used in these contexts would tell us very little about the *patterns* of subjection being indicated in these relationships. These patterns have to be discerned by looking at the overall thrust of the biblical message as it bears on these various contexts of authority.

It is not enough, then, simply to say that "the Bible tells wives to obey their husbands" or "the Bible tells citizens to obey the state." For example, in Ephesians 5:22 Paul tells wives to be subject to their husbands. But he prefaces this injunction with a guideline for both husbands and wives: "Be subject to one another out of reverence for Christ" (Eph. 5:21), and he goes on to tell husbands to love their wives "as Christ loved the church and gave himself up for her" (5:25). The directions to the husband here have the effect of revolutionizing the institution of marriage, as the institution was understood by the people to whom Paul was writing. Similarly, as we have seen, the biblical call for Christian citizens to be subject to political authority is consistently connected to an account of the proper task of the state: political authority is to punish wrongdoers and reward those who do right.

The proper pattern of subjection to authority is also regularly placed in a context of one's relationship to God. Wives and husbands are to submit to each other "out of reverence for Christ" (Eph. 5:21). And in 1 Peter 2 Christians are told to be subject to institutional authority "for the Lord's sake." This points to an important element in the Christian's posture of subjection. As we have already indicated, "subjection" does not require blind obedience to authority. Indeed, there will be times when the Christian community is called on to refuse to obey some law or policy laid down by institutional authority. But there must be an underlying respect for authority—that much seems clear from the New Testament passages on this subject.

There can be no denying a certain kind of "conservative" feel to the New Testament teaching on this topic. And the rationale for this attitude is not difficult to understand. Governments, at least as we know governments under sinful conditions, are necessitated by the fact of sin. The Bible is utterly realistic about the human capacity for duplicity, deceit, and disobedience. The biblical writers understand the need for discipline in human affairs. Sinful human beings need rules to live by, rules to which appropriate rewards and punishments are attached. One significant expression of this deep human need is the existence of the state, to which the power of "the sword" has been given.

Institutions, including political institutions, provide a much needed "ordering" of human life. And this good ordering occurs even when the government itself is less than perfect. We ought not to ignore this ordering function of government. Indeed, even under very wicked governments good things are provided: roads are built; zoning ordinances are in effect; communication networks are maintained; electricity, water, and other commodities are distributed. In short, even very wicked governments manage to protect human beings against certain varieties of chaos.

But this is not to say that Christians ought simply to approve of each and every government. Governments are indeed an important curb on human depravity, as has so often been argued; but they are also *affected* by that depravity. And the Bible never ignores the possibility that a government may itself be a terrible agent of human rebellion. This, again, is the message of Revelation 13, with its warnings against the beastly state.

When the Apostle tells us, then, that we are to be subject to government "for the Lord's sake," he is pointing to the element of *freedom* we have in submitting to institutional authority. Christian subjection is not something a government can assume will be automatically offered. It is something the Christian community offers voluntarily, in full consciousness that it is a choice we make before our Lord. And in making that choice, we are aware of the fact that our Lord has also warned us against bowing before beasts.

The Apostle has this freedom in mind when he adds these thoughts to his "subjection" injunction: "Live as free men, yet without using your freedom as a pretext for evil; but live as servants of God" (1 Pet. 2:16). We do have Christian freedom as over against the demands of government; and we ought to be aware of that freedom. But this freedom must never be used in such a way that it serves to rationalize evil actions. In effect, this puts the Christian community in a difficult position. Blind obedience is not acceptable; but neither is anarchy. To find the proper pattern of subjection within those boundaries is not an easy thing. It calls for an active searching out of the will of God for our political lives.

Four Commands

The necessary framework for searching out God's will in these matters is indicated in the form of four commands given in the final verse of our passage: "Honor all men. Love the brotherhood. Fear God. Honor the emperor" (1 Pet. 2:17). These injunctions have to be understood in relationship to the two societies in which Christians "in exile" find themselves. One pair of injunctions refers to the citizenry and authority structures of the Christian community proper, the new Israel: "Fear God." "Love the brotherhood." The other pair refers to "Babylon," to the larger human society in which the Christian community presently finds itself: "Honor the emperor." "Honor all men."

There is a clear ranking implied in the verbs used in these commands. The "fear" of God is the strongest. The "love" shown toward the members of the Christian community is an *agape*-love, a love that is self-sacrificing. The "honoring," on the other hand, which we are to offer both to the emperor and to "all men," is the weakest of the three verb terms used. Honoring is not fearing, nor is it *agape*-love; to honor, in the sense implied here, is to care for the well-being of those to whom the honor is offered.

We might think of our attitudes toward God and toward the Christian brotherhood and sisterhood as constituting the shape of our "domestic policy." The church, the new Israel, is our homeland; it is the theocratic community in which we have our primary citizenship. This citizenry is, of course, presently in dispersion. In our own time the theocratic community has its citizens spread through the world: there are Soviet Christians, British Christians, Ugandan Christians, Laotian Christians, and so on. But in spite of our dispersion we are bound together in one theocratic community over which Jesus is our Lord. Our domestic policy, then, toward this community is summarized along these lines: we must fear the Lord and love our fellow citizens in the community of Christ.

But what of our attitudes toward the various nations into which we are dispersed? How am I, a natural-born citizen of the United States, to relate to that social context? Or how is my friend Mark to relate to Britain, or my friend Patience to relate to South Africa? The Apostle offers these guidelines: honor the governments of these countries, while at the same time honoring all human beings who are fellow citizens in those places.

These guidelines in 1 Peter 2 are, I think, necessary for putting other biblical teachings in their proper context. Romans 13:7 describes our obligation to the state this way: "Honor to whom honor is due." To this 1 Peter 2 adds: and *only* honor for those to whom honor is due. We must not *fear* those to whom honor is due; nor must we *agape*-love them. And furthermore, we must honor *all* of those to whom honor is due—not only the emperor, but also all of those who are our fellow citizens in the nations in which we have our secondary citizenship.

This way of viewing things is helpful in understanding the cases of Christian civil disobedience mentioned earlier. Daniel could rightly defy the king's decree because the king was requiring people to fear him rather than to honor him. The early Christians could disobey laws banning Christian worship because they would not give to Caesar what properly belonged to God. Dutch Christians hid Jews in their "hiding places" because they realized that they were called to "honor all men."

Making Applications

At various points in this discussion of biblical passages I have made applications to contemporary situations. Strictly speaking, those applications should have been kept distinct from our interpretation of the biblical texts. In order to understand the relevance of the biblical message for us today, we must first attempt to understand its meaning for those to whom, and by whom, it was first articulated. But I do think that I have not made, in the process of interweaving exposition and application, any illegitimate applications to the contemporary situation.

In focusing on the question of what a text such as 1 Peter 2 means for contemporary Christians, we should be very clear that the passage we have discussed is itself an application of imagery and ideas from an earlier period to a contemporary situation. The Apostle is likening the situation of the first-century church to that of Israel in the dispersion. Just as Israel remained a distinct national people while scattered among the nations, so the first-century church is to view itself as a distinct people, dispersed into many places. Just as Israel was a theocratic community in exile, so the early church was to view itself as a chosen race, a holy nation, living out its time of exile with a clear sense of loyalty to the kingdom of Jesus.

It requires little imagination to extend the application a step further—into our own day. The church—not in a sense that limits "church" to a given ecclesiastical structure—is a community of persons who acknowledge the lordship of Christ over their lives. This acknowledgement, this confession of ultimate loyalty to the theo-

cratic community over which Jesus rules, binds all Christians together. This bond is stronger than any that is associated with national,
racial, or ethnic ties. There are, of course, other bonds and relationships that must be honored. But they must not be allowed to compete
with those ties that bind us to the kingdom of Jesus.

Recently I read a poignant letter written to North American Christians from a leader in one of the black churches in South Africa. He
told how a previously secret list had been published, revealing the
names of members of the *Broederbond,* or "Brotherhood," a South
African organization dedicated to promoting the interests of (white)
Afrikaners in racially troubled South Africa. This black Christian told
of the shock and hurt he experienced when he discovered that several
Christian persons whom he had trusted were members of this secret
organization. "Now we must confront them," he wrote, "and we
must ask them to choose between the brotherhood that they experience on the basis of their white blood and the brotherhood that comes
from being cleansed by the blood of Jesus."

That Christian man has touched on the heart of the issue for South
African Christians. A parallel challenge has to be faced by all Christians, especially lay Christians, today. What does it mean to belong to
the body of Jesus Christ? What does it mean to claim primary citizenship in a chosen race, a royal priesthood, a holy nation, God's own
people? What shall we do when that citizenship conflicts with American or British or South Korean or Soviet citizenship?

But this is still to formulate the problem in terms of "politics." In
fact, the challenges are much broader in scope. Peter tells the church
to "be subject for the Lord's sake to *every* human institution." And
we have seen that the subjection required here is not one of blind
obedience but of "honoring" those to whom honor is due. But Peter
was writing at a time when the state was an all-encompassing institution. The centuries between our day and his have been marked by
increasing "cultural differentiation." Institutional lines have come to
be much more clearly drawn. First-century readers would have had a
difficult time deciding, if asked, where, say, education stopped and
politics began; institutions had not yet "separated out" from one
another to the degree that they have today.

For contemporary Christians, then, it is not merely a question of
political authority. It is not just a question of how I will be subject to

the government of the United States or Canada or Mexico. Questions about subjection to "every institution" today also bear on many other areas in which rather clear patterns of institutional authority have evolved. And for many contemporary lay people these are where the crucial challenges emerge: In what ways, as a Christian employee, am I to be subject to those in authority at Corning Glass or ITT? Or, as a student or teacher, to the authorities at Harvard or Central City Junior College? Or to the powers that be in the Chamber of Commerce? Or in the NAACP? Or in the National Hockey League? How does sisterhood in Christ relate to sisterhood in the "consciousness-raising group"? How does brotherhood in Christ relate to the brotherhood of Teamsters? A fully adequate theology about, for, and by the laity will have to bridge the gap between the biblical message and these questions.

4

Some Questions

IN THE PRECEDING chapters we have covered quite a bit of territory. Many of the issues and themes with which we dealt will serve as the foundation for our further discussion about the nature and calling of the laity and their attempt to minister in the world. Readers will undoubtedly have questions about the ideas presented in the preceding chapters. In what follows I will attempt to anticipate possible questions and objections.

You talk a lot about politics. Don't you run the risk of "politicizing" the gospel?

This is an important concern. I would certainly not want to give the impression that the gospel is only, or primarily, a political message.

Those of us who are concerned with emphasizing the political dimensions of the biblical witness are often doing so in the awareness that many Christians assume, or even insist, that the gospel has *nothing* to do with politics. It is, therefore, possible that we go too far in the other direction, giving the impression that the gospel is primarily, or even solely, political.

But I believe that I have not given that impression in what I have written here. The gospel, as I understand it, is the good news about a Savior's love. To accept the gospel is to submit to the will of God as it is manifested in Jesus Christ, as he is presented to us in the Scriptures and as he is worshiped and obeyed by the community of his followers. But Jesus is more than a Savior—he is Lord and King. And I think that the recognition of his lordship and kingship has clear political dimensions. Similarly, the church is a fellowship of persons who are experiencing the redemptive love of Christ. But it is also more than that: it is a community of persons who are seeking to live out their lives in full obedience to the authority of God in Christ. This means that the church must consider what political, social, and economic obedience is. That is not, of course, the *whole* of the church's task. We must be obedient as parents, husbands, wives, partygoers, tennis players, theater attenders, and so on. But political obedience is one important, integral feature of the Christian life.

What do you mean by "politics"?

A whole book could be written in response to that question, since widely divergent accounts have been given by political theorists. I can offer only a brief account here.

The term *politics* is used to refer to at least three different matters. First, "politics" can refer to that domain in which government—civil government—is an obvious presence. To be concerned about politics in this sense is to focus one's attention on parliaments, political parties, mayors, prime ministers, presidents, senators, voting patterns, legislative budgets, and the like. There are important questions here about how far the domain of government ought to extend, or even about how far it does extend; but all of us have some kind of grasp of this area of social organization and interaction.

A second sense of "politics" has to do with a broader area. Here "political" issues can also be thought of as "social" issues. We can think here of the way in which Christians often talk about "social action." This sense may include "politics" in the first sense, but it also goes beyond that domain. Thus people who are engaged in environmental action programs, or in feminist groups, or in the area of race relations may be considered "political" activists, even though they may have little to do with legislative processes. Here "politics" has to do with the broad patterns of *public* life.

A third sense of "politics" has to do with authority patterns and processes of decision making, in a variety of spheres. We can think here of such terms as "sexual politics," "church politics," "university politics," "office politics." These terms often point to issues having to do with "who's boss," or "how to get things done," or "where the power is at," in a given institution or social group.

My references to "politics" in the preceding discussion are meant to cover all three of these senses. I believe that the gospel speaks to all these areas: the legislative process, broader concerns of public life, and the patterns of interaction in a variety of social settings.

You seem to want to reduce the authority of the clergy. Don't you think that the clergy person has a unique prophetic task, which ought not to be in any way undermined?

I don't want in any way to undermine the *legitimate* authority of the clergy. I agree that there is a certain kind of prophetic function associated with the ministry of preaching. But we have to understand that particular prophetic function in the larger context of prophetic ministries that are associated with the life and calling of the Christian community as such.

Basically, the Christian prophetic calling is exercised in two main areas. First, there is a prophetic calling that is exercised *within* the Christian community—a prophetic ministry by Christians to Christians. Second, there is a calling that is exercised on the part of the Christian community to a *larger* human community.

Let us take the second area first. The clergy has no unique function in the exercise of this kind of ministry. The question here is: "Who speaks prophetically on behalf of the church to the larger human community?" And the answer is: "Those Christians whose special calling it is to minister in the larger human community." Clergy may be involved in this ministry. Some clergy are hired by the church to engage in evangelism, counseling, or social work that brings them into regular contact—as a part of their primary work—with persons outside of the church. They must certainly engage in prophetic ministry in carrying out this work. And, of course, all or most clergy persons are also citizens and members of various communities in addition to their work in the institutional church; they must bring prophetic sensitivities to those roles.

But none of that distinguishes them from lay persons. The laity too are involved in ministries in the larger human community. They, too, have roles and functions in various communities and institutions. They, too, must bring prophetic sensitivities to their work in the world.

The other area has to do with a prophetic ministry within the Christian community. Here the ordained ministry has a very special role. Clergy persons are called to equip the laity for ministry in the world. And this task of equipping is, among other things, a prophetic one. It is often said that the prophet has two functions, to "fore-tell" and "forth-tell." I am thinking of the latter dimension in speaking of the "prophetic" here: the task of "telling forth."

The clergy person whose primary work is in the areas of preaching, sacraments, pastoral functions, and church administration must carry these jobs out with prophetic sensitivities. He or she must certainly not simply tell the laity "what they want to hear." Prophetic preaching will often include admonition, criticism, and warning; it will often be characterized by a clear and bold "Thus saith the Lord!" Here the ordained minister resembles the Old Testament prophet, authoritatively bringing God's Word to the people of God.

I do not want to undermine this prophetic task in any way. The clergy perform a very special function in the community of God's people. They possess an authority deriving from their special training, their vocation, their gifts, and the fact that they have been singled out by the believing community for the performance of certain tasks.

But we must not assume that the prophetic ministry that takes place within the Christian community is the unique calling of the clergy. All of us—clergy and laity—ought to admonish and correct one another. Prophetic "forth-telling" can take place within the family, at the church coffee hour, in the Sunday school class, in bull sessions and heated arguments. The clergy are called to *lead* the church in its "internal" prophetic ministry. They are called to occupy a *special* place in the exercise of that ministry. But they do not have an exclusive franchise on that ministry.

I must also add that my discussion of the role of the clergy is not designed as an attack on ordained ministers or priests. I would guess that a vast majority of the clergy agree with what I have written here. They do not want to be considered *the* "ministers" of the church. They realize that the laity has a ministerial calling. Unfortunately, however, many lay people have misconceptions and false expectations regarding the clergy. The danger today in the church is not so much that the clergy will misunderstand the nature of their own calling; it is that the laity will misunderstand the proper role of the clergy and will thereby refuse to accept their own responsibility for ministry in the world.

In the light of the Christian community's tendency toward arrogance, shouldn't we drop the phrase "people of God" altogether?

I like the phrase "people of God" because it seems to be a profound biblical conception. I would not want to argue that we ought to use biblical language today in an uncritical manner. For example, both Isaiah and the Psalmist talk about being washed as "white as snow." Even though this sort of comment, in its biblical setting, has absolutely no racial connotations, I am very reluctant to sing hymns that use that kind of language, just because it can be so easily misunderstood.

But the phrase "people of God" is a very *central* biblical notion. It refers to the corporate nature of our life and calling—an important antidote to the rugged individualism that has so often crept into Christian thinking. And, as I have already argued, it speaks in a prophetic way to those who are caught up in false quests for "people-hood." It tells them that on the deepest level a true sense of "belonging" can be found only by being joined to that company of persons who can rejoice in the fact that their sins are forgiven. Properly understood, this phrase points to a profound alternative to racism, superpatriotism, and other forms of idolatry centering on some pattern of group identification.

There is also a very basic point of theology at stake here. I believe that biblical orthodoxy requires us to acknowledge the distinction between the "saved" and the "unsaved," between those who have openly committed themselves to be followers of Jesus and those who have not. This is not to say that *I* can always tell the difference in an easy fashion; in the end it will be the Lord, and only the Lord, who will be able to separate the sheep from the goats. But nonetheless, whether a person has made a commitment to follow Jesus is a crucial matter; ultimately, it is the most important issue any human being faces. Belonging to "the people of God" is not something that should occasion pride or boasting, but it is a matter of the utmost importance.

Do you really mean to imply that evangelistic methodologies and programs that attempt to be apolitical are not worthy of being called "evangelism"?

I have no desire to attack such programs as being "pseudo evangelism." I do have fears that these programs are often very "hit-and-miss'' in their emphasis and that they often stress what I consider to be an overreliance on "formulas" for evangelization.

It is precisely because of my fear of "formulas" that I would *not* want all evangelism to be overtly "political" in nature. If one is attempting to bring the gospel to persons who are burdened with considerable guilt, or struggling with alcoholism, or going through a painful divorce, it would probably be silly or even cruel to begin arguing with them about race relations or Cuban socialism. We have to meet people where they are and bring the gospel to them at those places where we find an openness to the message of redeeming love.

If, then, I were evangelizing a man who is struggling with alcoholism and who also happens to be fond of making disparaging remarks about black welfare mothers, I would not concentrate on his racial and economic views. To have him arrive at the point where he can turn his struggle with alcoholism over to a loving God, to have him experience the power of the cross in his very personal struggle—these would be crucial concerns. But—and I must stress this—the process of evangelism is not *complete* until he confronts his own pride and arrogance in the areas of economics and race relations. It may take a long time before we can begin to work on those issues, but we ought to want to bring him to that point.

However, in other cases the political dimension may be the very first matter to be addressed. In witnessing to Marxists or young university radicals or alienated black persons, we may have to begin by presenting Jesus as liberator and King. The question is not *whether* evangelism has political dimensions. It does. The question is a tactical one, having to do with when a given individual can best be confronted with the political claims of the gospel.

Doesn't talk about being "in exile," or being "pilgrims in a foreign land," encourage a "pie-in-the-sky" kind of Christianity?

Unfortunately, these themes have often been associated with an attitude of cultural withdrawal. This is especially true among the Protestant fundamentalists. Many of them believe that the world is in the process of degeneration, that things will get worse and worse until the world will finally be destroyed. But this does not trouble them in any ultimate sense because they believe that they are bound for heaven. Indeed, on one very common fundamentalist pattern of

thought all the true Christians will be taken out of the world before the
final showdown. Thus their sense of alienation from the present order
of things goes hand in hand with the attitudes of cultural pessimism
and passive withdrawal from responsible involvement in society.

What I see as being wrong with that position is not that those
fundamentalists have utilized the exile and pilgrimage themes as
such, but that they have interpreted them in such a way that they
reinforce cultural withdrawal. I have my own theories about why
fundamentalism went in this direction. There were various historical
reasons why fundamentalists became disillusioned with large institutions and why they developed rather strong hostilities toward certain
aspects of the dominant culture. In short, I think that the pattern of
cultural withdrawal is not intrinsically related to these themes.

Indeed, as I have insisted, God's pilgrim people in their biblical
setting are called to perform good works, to seek the welfare of the
city in which they are living. It seems clear from the biblical materials
that the condition of being in exile does not rule out an active,
aggressive interest in promoting justice and righteousness.

There is also the question of what we are alienated *from*. We are not
alienated from the *creation* as Christians. What we are alienated from
is the sinful order, the distortions of the good creation that presently
prevail in human societies. The fundamentalists like to sing, "This
world is not my home." I agree with that sentiment as stated. But we
must also be able to sing, "This is my Father's world." Is there a
contradiction here? I think not. In each case the term *world* refers to
something different. The "world" that is not my home is the sinful
order. The "world" that still belongs to God is the good creation. The
Christian quest, then, is to refuse to identify with the rule of sin and to
live out our loyalties to the Reign of Jesus, which is the restoration
and fulfillment of the good creation.

I must also repeat my concern that the biblical references to
"exile" not be used to reinforce the idea that everything that occurs in
the larger human society is to be viewed as evil or "pagan." Christians are to understand their "alien" status in such a way that they do
not offer their ultimate allegiance to the status quo. But it is also
possible to discern and encourage and promote "signs" of the coming
kingdom in the larger societies in which we presently live. We must
not simply view these societies as "barren lands" from which we

should want to escape as quickly as possible. Indeed, we are called to identify with all that is good in those societies. Nothing that I have said should be taken as promoting the idea that we are not responsible for our cultural surroundings.

But I must also confess that I always feel some ambivalence when people criticize "pie in the sky" religion. I don't think that we will feel fully "at home" until the transformation and renewal occur as described in Revelation 21:5: "Behold, I make all things new." The Christian hope is directed toward the future return of Christ as victorious King. This hope is intimately connected to a sense that the promised renewal is "not yet." I don't know if that means that our "pie" is in the "sky," but it certainly has a "by-and-by" feel to it.

Even if the church is in some sense a "Christian nation," can't we also speak of contemporary countries, such as the United States, as "Christian nations"?

My main concern in arguing that the church is a Christian nation is to point out that our loyalties as Christians move along lines that go beyond what we currently think of as "national" borders. I am both a Christian and a United States citizen. It seems perfectly clear to me that my identity as a Christian overrides anything that may be imposed on me by virtue of my American citizenship. When someone tells me that I ought to do such and such *because* I am an American, I can only respond that my loyalties to black South African Methodists, and Russian Pentecostals and Latin American Catholic peasants make stronger demands on me than those that flow from my commitments to the land of my birth.

I was at a meeting recently at which someone said, "We Americans should stay out of South Africa's internal affairs. We've got enough problems of our own to occupy us." That kind of comment is not *totally* off the mark. It is often easier to show a concern about injustices that occur on the other side of the world than to become involved in dealing with problems in our own neighborhoods. But the rationale implicit in that remark will not do. If Christians are being mistreated in South Africa, or if Christians are *doing* the mistreating in South Africa, it *is* my problem. I am not saying that there are no other reasons for caring about what happens in South Africa. I am certainly not saying that we ought not to care about the mistreatment of or by non-Christians, or that I have no legitimate interest in the situation as an American citizen and consumer. But I am arguing that at the very least—even if there were no other grounds for concern—I ought to be concerned about the well-being of the dispersed members of the body of Christ in South Africa.

Now the problem is complicated, as the question indicates, by the fact that some citizens of various countries think of their own national communities as "Christian nations." One possible way of responding to this phenomenon is simply to say that there are various senses of "Christian nation." The United States, for example, might be thought of as a "Christian nation" in the sense that many of its cultural patterns have been influenced by the historical development of Christian life and thought, by Christian ideals. This is, for the most part, an empirical contention, and I suspect that there is something that could be said for it, although I would want to quarrel with some of the claims that have been made on its behalf.

The main problem is that talk about this or that country's being a "Christian nation" has often been associated with a very arrogant understanding of the nation's role in the community of nations. People come to think of their nation as a "chosen people," with a special calling to pursue in the world, and this has often led to the worst sort of imperialism, where "heathen" peoples are subdued with a missionary zeal.

I have often heard North American Christians apply 2 Chronicles 7:14 to the contemporary United States: "If my people who are called by my name humble themselves, and pray and seek my face, and turn from their wicked ways, then I will hear from heaven, and will forgive their sins and heal their land." This promise, I think, cannot be applied to the United States. It is a promise to Old Testament Israel, whose counterpart today is the church of Christ. When we hear "my people" here, we must think of the Christian community, it is to that community that divine healing is promised.

If we want biblical promises that can be applied to the United States, we must turn to the exile literature of the Bible. Daniel 4:27 is a good example. There Daniel, living in exile in Babylon but serving in the court of the pagan king, offers this word of hope to the king: "Therefore, O king, let my counsel be acceptable to you, break off your sins by practicing righteousness, and your iniquities by showing mercy to the oppressed, that there may perhaps be a lengthening of your tranquility."

Note the differences between these two conditional promises: if Israel will engage in national repentance and repair her ways, God will heal her land, but Babylon is asked to practice righteousness and to show mercy to the oppressed, with the promise of a possible lengthening of her tranquility. It is the latter pattern and promise that we can hold out to specific nations today.

The ruling elite of South Africa consider their country to be a "Christian nation." Certain religious denominations have a powerful influence on governmental thinking, and the political self-understanding of the ruling class is shot through with religious symbols and concepts. Yet the patterns of political, economic, and cultural life in South Africa are profoundly unjust. If the religious veneer of Afrikaner thought and practice were to fade away and South African society were to become a much more just society, I would consider it to be more of a "Christian nation" than it presently is. In the final analysis, talk about South Africa or the United States as "Christian nations" seems to me not to come to much. The important question is whether those societies are characterized by a just order.

If we know that the reign of Christ is not going to come as a result of our "good works," why perform them?

The social, political, and economic good works that we perform serve a number of purposes. First and foremost, they are a part of our obedient response to the gospel. The Christian community ought not to be concerned primarily with success but with faithfulness. One good reason, then, for performing good works is that we have been commanded to do so.

But if that were all there was to say about things, it would be much like the situation in which the teacher tells the class to keep counting by tens while she is out of the room: we know what to do but we're not sure why we were told to do it. Fortunately, in our case we can get some indications, both from the Scriptures and from history, as to why we are to perform good works. From the past experience of the Christian community we learn that faithful Christian action, even when it goes against prevailing opinions, is sometimes blessed with success. While we cannot expect our efforts to lead to the establishment of a utopian society, there is no reason why we cannot look for breakthroughs in the area of justice and righteousness. We should not expect the kingdom in its fullness to come as a result of our actions, but we can hope for "signs" and "firstfruits" of the kingdom.

But we can also labor in the legitimate hope that our efforts will be vindicated and rewarded at the Judgment. Peter says that the "Gentiles" will "see your good deeds and glorify God on the day of visitation."

If the church is the "new Israel," what does this mean for the Jewish people today? After all, there is actually a nation named "Israel" in existence today.

This is a difficult subject, which, as far as I can tell, is clouded in considerable mystery. There are some contemporary Christian thinkers who think that God still has a redemptive plan for the Jewish people as a nation, a plan that is distinct from his designs for gentile Christianity. This view is not only defended with great vigor by many fundamentalists who accept dispensationalist theology, but also has been put forth by theologians with significant ecumenical reputations.

I am not inclined toward such a view. As I read the New Testament, it seems clear that Israel has been opened to the Gentiles, thus becoming a new spiritual entity made up of all and only those who trust in the redemptive work of Christ. In my view—and there is some irony in this—Christian Arabs and Christian Palestinian refugees are members of the "true" Israel. To be "pro-Israel" in a New Testament sense, then, is to advocate the rights of Middle East Christians.

In saying that, I do not want to rule out the possibility that God may still have an attitude of special favor toward the "natural" daughters and sons of Abraham, Isaac, and Jacob. But even if that is the case, I believe that we must invite all human beings, Jew and Gentile alike, to acknowledge Jesus as the Promised One of Israel. And I most certainly believe that God requires Jews today, as he did of old, to act justly toward their neighbors and to show mercy to the oppressed.

I do not mean to pretend that these brief comments can do justice to a very complicated topic. And I must hasten to add that nothing I have said is meant to reinforce the ugly phenomenon of anti-Semitism which has so often appeared in Western, and even Christian, history. The shadow of the Holocaust is still all too visible for any of us to want to contribute in any way to any further suffering on the part of Jewish people. Christians must take seriously the New Testament emphasis on the church as the New Israel. We must also pray for peace on behalf of the modern nation of Israel, a peace that is achieved within the framework of justice. But in all of this we must be acutely aware of the vicious crimes and hatred that have often characterized Christian actions toward Jewish people.

5

What Is God Up To?

THUS FAR we have been dealing, for the most part, with generalities. This will make some lay people uneasy—or at least this has been my experience. When an academic such as I am has occasion to speak to a group of lay people, this is a very common complaint: "But you're just talking in generalities. What does all of this mean where the rubber hits the road? What exactly are you telling us to *do?*"

In all honesty I can respond to a complaint of that sort only by insisting that we are dealing with an area in which it is very difficult to be specific in offering guidance. In a previous chapter I indicated that theology *for* the laity must be, in an important sense, theology *by* the laity. No philosopher or theologian or economist can simply tell a waitress or a florist or a real-estate agent what to "do," where the "doing" involves very specific life situations. How the Christian gospel is to be lived out in the context of specific vocations is a matter that must finally be decided by those who experience those vocations in a concrete, day-to-day manner.

But, having admitted that, I would also plead that the waitresses and florists and real-estate agents not sell "generalities" short. In order to apply concerns to practical situations, there must be certain things that *are* applied. What the Christian will want to apply are principles, theologically grounded convictions, the claims of the gospel. So, in order to make our applications properly, we must first have our principles, convictions, and claims straight. We must submit to the discipline of careful reflection on those "generalities" that we must bring to bear on our work in the world.

Sometimes, then, the "What are we to *do?*" complaint-question comes too early in the process. North Americans especially are often caught up by a kind of "pragmatist" spirit that spurns disciplined reflection. The important thing, in this way of viewing matters, is to "get things done"; there is little use for ideas unless they have practical consequences that are immediately obvious.

Those Christians who are attracted toward this pragmatist spirit would do well to attend to the fact that the Bible regularly stresses the need for times of reflection in preparation for ministry. The prophets spent long periods in the wilderness. Jesus engaged in prayer and fasting for forty days in the desert before embarking on his redemptive ministry. Considerable time between Paul's conversion and his work as an apostle was devoted to instruction and meditation.

Contemporary lay people, too, need to submit to the discipline of reflection and "detached" discussion of their own assumptions and principles in the light of the biblical message. There is much wisdom in the old saw about the people who "can't see the forest for the trees." It is important that Christians be aware of overall *patterns:* the patterns of the biblical message and the patterns of our own actual involvement in the world.

Discernment

A friend of mine was once in a strange city on business, and one evening he noticed in a newspaper announcement that a noted theologian was giving a public lecture on the subject "The Work of Jesus Christ." Since he was free that evening, he attended the lecture. The theologian mainly reviewed the key elements in the biblical portrayal of the redemptive mission of Jesus. During the question period afterward a young man addressed the theologian as follows: "Sir, I heard you tell us about some important dimensions of the work of Christ. You spoke of how Jesus was the fulfillment of Old Testament prophecy. You gave an account of his birth, his earthly ministry, and his death and resurrection. You also gave stirring expression to your own conviction that Jesus will someday return as victorious King. But, sir, there is one thing I'm still not very clear about: What exactly is Jesus doing right now?"

A similar question is raised by Marcus Borg in his book on social change. Borg asks: "What is God up to?" (Marcus Borg, *Conflict and Social Change,* page 54). This is an important question: What is God up to today? Where is he at work in the forces of change on the contemporary scene? If we could get clear about this matter, we would then be in a position to decide how we as contemporary Christians can better bring our own actions and programs into conformity to his will.

This question about God's activities in the present world is closely related to what the Bible says about *discernment*. In 1 Corinthians 12, in his list of the "gifts of the Spirit," the Apostle refers to "the ability to distinguish between spirits" (v. 10). And in Romans 12:2, Paul warns us, "Do not be conformed to this world, but be transformed by the renewal of your mind, that you may prove what is the will of God, what is good and acceptable and perfect."

The way in which Paul formulates the matter in this verse from Romans 12 establishes a rather direct link between the question of discernment and our previous discussion. We Christians are called, as we have already argued at length, to perform "good works." In Romans 12 Paul tells us that we have to "*prove* what is the will of God, what is good and acceptable and perfect" (the italics are mine). We are not simply required to engage in whatever strikes us as "good works." Our good works must be in conformity with the will of God; and we must struggle to prove, or to discern, what God's will is, so that our actions may be "good and acceptable and perfect."

Or, as the case is formulated in the verse just cited from 1 Corinthians 12, we must "distinguish between spirits." There are various "spirits" or minds at work in the world. We must be extremely careful not to be conformed to forces that are at variance with the will of God. That is why there is such a strong emphasis in the New Testament (expressed in many different ways) on the need to test the spirits.

Few Christians would want to quarrel with this emphasis on the need for discernment. We are all aware that we daily encounter cultural forces that, if we were to give in to them, would destroy our faith. Pornographic magazines, books advocating "sexual freedom," TV programs that show open contempt for a commitment to marital fidelity—these represent forces that assault biblical standards of sexual morality. We are also continuously bombarded in the mass media by advertising that attempts to stimulate greed and envy with regard to material possessions.

Most Christians would agree on the threats that arise in these areas of sexuality and consumer patterns. But on matters having to do with forces for change in other areas, there would be considerable dis-agreement. What about the "spirits" that are at work in the areas of race relations, male-female roles, economics, national politics? How, if at all, are we to discern the will of God with regard to these matters? How, with reference to such things, are we to "prove . . . what is good and acceptable and perfect"?

God's Action in Current Struggles

In January 1976 a group of Christian leaders from the Boston area issued a statement called "The Boston Affirmations." Of the many documents and credos produced by Christian groups in recent years, this statement is perhaps the most straightforward in linking the will of God in a positive way with various social movements that are at work in the human community.

The opening words of the Affirmations immediately strike this note of identification: "The living God is active in current struggles to bring a Reign of Justice, Righteousness, Love, and Peace." The document goes on to apply some biblical concepts to contemporary social themes, and it lists some of the resources available for the contemporary situation from a variety of Christian traditions. Then, under the subtitle, "Present Witnesses," it introduces a list of twelve areas of contemporary social struggle, prefacing the list with these words: "The transforming reality of God's reign is found today"— and then following with a list of twelve areas of concern. Here are a few of the items listed:

> —In the struggles of the poor to gain a share of the world's wealth, to become creative participants in the common economic life, and to move our world toward an economic democracy of equity and accountability.
>
> —In the transforming drive for ethnic dignity against the persistent racism of human hearts and social institutions.
>
> —In the endeavor by women to overcome sexist subordination in the church's ministry, in society at large, and in the images that bind our minds and bodies.

Among other areas mentioned are patterns of family life, a concern for cities, health care, attitudes toward the nation, technology, the arts, legal justice, and then, finally:

—And especially in those branches and divisions of the church where the truth is spoken in love, where transforming social commitments are nurtured and persons are brought to informed conviction, where piety is renewed and recast in concert with the heritage, and where such struggles as those here identified are seen as the action of the living God who alone is worshiped.

These Affirmations provide us with a clear, and relatively unambiguous, example of the way in which some Christians claim to discern "what God is up to" in the broader reaches of contemporary society. Why do the writers of the Boston Affirmations say what they do? On what basis do they claim to discern the biblical God at work in the movements and struggles they mention? They do give some account of their thinking in this regard. But before examining their views any further, we would do well to look briefly at some alternative perspectives.

Pious Agnosticism

There are many Christians who would be profoundly uneasy with the views set forth in the Boston Affirmations. It is not that they would simply disagree with the Boston group over this or that item in their list of movements in which God is active. I am thinking here of Christians who have very basic disagreements with the fundamental perspective as such of the Boston group.

One such alternative viewpoint I will label "pious agnosticism." The word *agnostic* comes from the Greek word *agnosto,* which means literally "I don't know." We commonly use the label "agnostic" to refer to people who claim not to know whether or not there is a God. But the term can be used to describe any position that involves a profession of ignorance on some topic. Here I mean to use the term to apply to those Christians who would disagree with the Boston document because they claim not to know what God is up to in his workings in the larger human society. And I call them *pious* agnostics because they give the impression that it is a special mark of piety or spirituality to profess ignorance on that subject.

I don't know whether anyone consistently holds to this position of pious agnosticism. But we can certainly find hints of it here and there in the Christian community. If someone did hold to the position consistently, it would be expressed along these lines. God works, it would be argued, in mysterious ways. He is bringing his purposes to fruition in the world, but in a manner that passes human understanding. It is not our business, then, as humans to inquire into his secret workings in the world. God has told us what he wants us to know by revealing his will to us in the Scriptures. The Bible contains his "revealed will." But there is also much that he has not revealed to us; he also has a secret or "hidden will." We must be content with what he has revealed to us. We must not attempt to probe his secret workings.

Note that this line of thought does not involve a denial that God is at work in the world. On the contrary, pious agnostics want to insist that God is at work in everything that comes to pass in human history. If you were to ask them what God is up to in the contemporary world, you could expect an answer along these lines: he is up to *everything!*

Well, then, does that mean that God approves equally of all that happens in the world? Does it mean that he is not only working in favor of women's liberation and the struggle against racism, but is also supporting the forces of sexism and racism? The pious agnostic would respond in the negative. In one sense God is in control of everything. But that does not mean that everything that happens has his blessing. Some things he allows in order to bring judgment on sin, or to allow human beings to work out the implications of their evil choices. But there are other things that he positively endorses; these movements conform to his good, saving purposes in the world.

The pious agnostic would say all these things. But if we were to ask which of the groups at work in the contemporary world have aims endorsed by God, the pious agnostic would profess not to know. Pious agnostics know *that* God is working out his will through these movements, but they do not know *how* he is doing so. They do not pretend to grasp his specific intentions as he works out his providential will in human history. Indeed, they view it as sinful to *attempt* to "psych out" God in his mysterious dealings with the human race.

There is much to be said in favor of pious agnosticism. Of course there are matters that God has hidden from us. And, if so, it would be foolish and pretentious, if not sinful, to probe into areas which God wants to remain mysterious. The rub comes, of course, when Christians profess ignorance where they ought *not* to be ignorant. The important questions, then, are: What should Christians say about the patterns of social change? What does the Word reveal to us that might equip us to exercise the gift of discernment with regard to the sorts of struggles mentioned in the Boston Affirmations?

There doesn't seem to be any clear way of drawing lines in a way that allows us to say, "God's word tells us about this kind of thing, but not about that kind of thing." There are areas in our personal lives in which it is rather easy to discern the will of God; but there are other personal matters in which it is often very difficult to discern his will. The same holds for "corporate" questions. We can say without reticence that God did not approve of Hitler's *Reich,* nor did he approve of the atrocities committed by Idi Amin. On the other hand, it may not be as easy to tell what God thinks about, or what he is attempting to bring about through, the present policies of the Nigerian government or the last federal election in Canada.

We might put the case this way, then. Pious agnosticism is a proper attitude where we are legitimately ignorant of God's hidden purposes, but it is improper where we have the resources to discern his workings in history. And there is no way of partitioning off whole areas of life from Christian discernment. It is not the case that God's dealings with us on a purely personal level are an open book, while his workings in the corporate patterns of society are completely hidden. Some of God's personal dealings with us are quite easy to discern; others are difficult. And the same holds for events on the corporate level.

Social Dualism

There is a second group of Christians who would disagree strongly with the Boston Affirmations. They would also dissent from the views of the pious agnostics. Unlike the agnostics, this group would insist that we can discern the workings of God in the broad patterns of our culture. But these Christians would profess to discern something very different from what is described in the Boston Affirmations.

I am thinking here of the tendency on the part of some Christians to view the workings of God in history in terms of a rather stark dualism between "church" and "world." This dualistic view shows up in many forms; it can be found on both the "left" and the "right" of the contemporary Christian community. I will concentrate here on the "leftist" version.

My brief account of this position here will be overdrawn. I know of no Christian thinker who would put the case in the stark terms I will use. But there is a certain kind of "Christian radicalism" today that tends in this direction, and in describing the view I will follow the tendency to its extreme.

The present world, in this view, is under the domain of demonic "principalities and powers," spiritual forces that serve as the "false gods" of contemporary social life. These forces are at work in the cultural arena, and their presence is manifested in the form of various "isms" that dominate the cultural patterns of Western society, such as consumerism, racism, sexism, militarism, nationalism, and imperialism. These "isms" are the facts of social life in the world in which we live. To grow up in Argentina, or Canada, or India, or Switzerland is to come under the domination of these powers.

The influence of these powers is pervasive, and from a human point of view it would seem hopeless to counter them in any way. But the Bible teaches that Jesus has already defeated them: "He disarmed the principalities and powers and made a public example of them, triumphing over them in him" (Col. 2:15). On the cross, the principalities and powers were defeated. They have not been eliminated from the scene, but their doom is sealed, their death warrant has been made out. The powers, and the dominant social structures over which they have control, are headed for destruction.

Another thing also happened as a result of the cross. A new social entity has been introduced into human affairs: the church, the community of Christ followers. This community lives in the awareness that the powers are defeated. Christians are called to stand "over against" the principalities and powers, witnessing to their doomed status: "If with Christ you died to the elemental spirits of the universe, why do you live as if you still belonged to the world?" (Col. 2:20). This community is called to live in radical opposition to the powers, showing forth a new and better way of living together as human beings. The church, in this view, is on the side of history. Even though it looks as if the radical Christians are out of step with the ways things are progressing, they are, in fact, on the winning side. It is their calling to live out their communal life in radical obedience to the One who has been victorious over the principalities and powers.

Sometimes proponents of this view, or this tendency, put the case in terms of the metaphors of "life" and "death." The sinful structures of corporate life today are involved in "the way of death." They are devoted to disintegration and destruction. The Christian community, on the other hand, represents "the way of life." To those who lack the gift of discernment, it may appear at times that there are improvements, signs of life, in the larger society. But this is misleading. The corporate structures will not improve; they are corrupt in the very core of their being. Similarly, it may seem at times that the Christian community is on a hopeless course, or is suffering severe setbacks. But this, too, is illusion. The victory belongs to those who oppose the dominant structures.

What, then, is God up to in the contemporary world? Two basic things, in fact: he is allowing the structures to pursue their way of death, and he is preparing his faithful people to celebrate the victory. In this view the Christian community is not required to attempt to change things in the larger community; indeed, that would be futile. They are called to be a faithful community, living in resistance to the principalities and powers—and calling others to join them in their resistance.

We can see how this tendency, if carried to the extreme, would provide an alternative to the perspective of the Boston Affirmations. The Boston group discerns signs of "life" beyond the boundaries of the Christian community. It offers hope to the larger community, if only people will endorse the forces for good that are at work in the world. This is what the radical dualist would want to argue against. There is no hope apart from that community that openly celebrates the victory of Jesus.

There is much to be said in favor of the views associated with this dualistic position. The Bible does talk about "principalities and powers," and it is important that Christians resist the influence of these powers as the powers shape the values, goals, and attitudes of the human community. (Readers who wish to pursue this topic are encouraged to read Hendrik Berkhof's excellent study *Christ and the Powers.*) In fact, there is often a strongly dualistic "feel" to the way in which the Bible views history; this is especially true of apocalyptic writings, such as the book of Revelation. History *is* a struggle between good and evil, between the designs of God and the designs of

Satan. And Satan's forces *are* doomed. In the end, the Lamb of God will be the victorious conqueror.

The problem is not so much with seeing the world in terms of a struggle between two forces. The real difficulty lies in identifying just where those forces are at work. Here is where some of us will have problems with the views of the radical dualists. For my part, I am convinced that there are forces for justice and righteousness at work beyond the borders of the Christian community. And I am equally convinced that the forces of Satan occasionally penetrate the Christian community, even the "radical Christian" community.

Under present conditions, then, there can be no case made for the idea of a pure church at work in a hopelessly evil world. Both church and world are a battleground where the struggle is taking place. Indeed, each of us is a miniature battleground—the struggle takes place within the life of each Christian.

Shattering Barriers

It seems to me that neither of these alternative views holds up as providing adequate objections to the perspective of the Boston Affirmations. God *is* at work in the world, bringing about his goals in history. There are movements on the contemporary scene to which Christians ought to offer some sort of word of approval.

But *which* movements? As we Christians observe (and participate in) contemporary affairs, what shall we look for as we attempt to discern the will of God in the midst of the forces for change?

The Boston group does offer some guidelines on this matter. They have not simply chosen a list of movements in an arbitrary manner and "baptized" them as Christian causes. In words that we have already quoted, the Boston Affirmations state that God "is active in current struggles to bring a Reign of Justice, Righteousness, Love and Peace." And elsewhere in the document the writers note that God works through the kind of activity that "shatters the barriers of ethnic, class, familial, national and caste restrictions."

These are helpful observations, and they do give us some guidelines to work with. The God of the Scriptures is concerned about "Justice, Righteousness, Love and Peace"; he is a God who is devoted to "shattering barriers." So, as we observe the contemporary scene, we can ask ourselves where we see these concerns being promoted. And we can expect that God is at work in special ways wherever people are working to bring about just, righteous, loving, and peaceful relations, wherever barriers are being broken down.

But at a second glance things may not be so simple. For one thing, we will have to get beyond the rhetoric these movements often use in order to examine the substance of the claims made by social movements. An appeal to "love" has been used in recent years to promote a variety of causes—for example, by the "flower children" and by advocates of "free love." Both sides in the abortion debate want "justice," as do both critics and defenders of affirmative action programs.

And what about "shattering barriers"? Is it simply the case that God is active wherever "barriers" are being broken down? Members of hippie communes wanted to break down barriers, as did the advocates of the drug culture. So do the defenders of "open marriage" and the promoters of "gay rights." It is not enough to be opposed to every kind of barrier. Not every curb on our sinful impulses, not every rule or restriction, is a "barrier" that ought to be shattered. God is not opposed to everything that might be called a "barrier"; he is opposed to those barriers that thwart his purposes. But it is not always easy to distinguish those barriers that ought to be removed from those that are necessary in human affairs.

The Need for Tentativeness

Another concern has been raised by Lewis Smedes in an article ("From Hartford to Boston," *The Reformed Journal,* April 1976) in which he discusses the Boston Affirmations. Smedes writes:

> Boston says we can *know* where the kingdom is, check off the places, make a list, point to movements and struggles and say, "Lo, here," and "not there" . . . .
> But how do we really know for sure? What prevents another group of people from making another list: the kingdom of God is found today wherever decent people struggle for law and order, wherever people work to increase respect for authority, wherever people are laboring to extend American democracy?

These are good questions, especially because the examples Smedes offers are not completely off the mark from the perspective of Christian social concern. As we noted in an earlier chapter, the Bible shows some preference for "order" and lawful behavior. Christians can be genuine advocates of just and righteous changes in the social order and yet have genuine fears about the effects of violent and radical social change.

Some of the problems that arise in this area have to do with a gap between a commitment to certain goals and a commitment to specific programs that are put forth for achieving those goals. I can be fully committed to the goal of a just society in South Africa and yet not be happy with the actual program set forth by some guerrilla group for achieving that goal. Or I may be fully committed to full equality for women and yet have legitimate concerns about the effects of putting children in the hands of government-sponsored "day care" programs.

Smedes's questions point to the fact that more concerns go into Christian discernment than those mentioned by the Boston group. When the full range of Christian concerns is brought to bear on our decision-making, the issues can become complicated. Thus, Smedes goes on to ask:

> Do we not, in fact, have to say that *it seems to us* that this or that struggle embodies sufficient kingdom goals and *seems* to use means that are at least consistent enough with kingdom norms to deserve our involvement? And do we not always have to accept the reservation that we might be wrong? And even where we might be right, is there not always enough human obfuscation and human duplicity in all our efforts that they deny even as they signal the promise of God's kingdom?

Note that Smedes is *not* suggesting that the Boston group is misguided in attempting to discern the workings of God among contemporary social movements. Nor is he simply rejecting the list of movements that are mentioned in the Boston document. But he is asking for a note of tentativeness in our attempts to identify the reign of Christ in the contemporary social scene.

Perhaps we have a clue here as to what constitutes a proper alternative to pious agnosticism: it may be that what we need is not so much pious agnosticism as *pious tentativeness*. Our attempts to identify specific movements with the will of God should be tentative and conditional. We should leave room for revision and qualification in our endorsements. This does not mean that we ought not to *look* aggressively for the workings of God in the world. We *must* actively seek to discern his will, to "prove . . . what is good and acceptable and perfect." But the task of "proving" is a difficult one. And when we have not fulfilled that task, we would do well to utilize the "it seems to us . . ." clause, as Smedes suggests.

In a manner similar to that of the pious agnostics we must acknowledge some element of "hiddenness" in God's workings in the world. God is presently bringing about his redemptive purposes throughout society; he is at work implementing his designs amid the processes of social change. But we must exercise caution in our attempts to discern his movements in history.

The Role of Christian Community

The dualist rightly stresses the central role of Christian community as we attempt to live in obedience to God's will. God has called together a people, and he has given them his Word to serve as a light and a lamp on their pilgrimage. The community of Christian disciples is the context in which that Word must be interpreted. The gifts of the Spirit, including the gift of discernment, are given to the community; individuals and groups receive these gifts in order to build up the whole body for that obedience.

Discernment is, then, a communal act. It is not something that occurs primarily through mystical experiences; it occurs best when the community of God's people are willing to study and discuss and argue together about what God is doing in the world. This does involve a "withdrawal" of sorts from the world. A proper understanding of God's providential workings can be gained only by experiencing the redemption that is to be found in the midst of God's people. But this experience is only the beginning of cultural discernment; for, having turned away from the world to taste the firstfruits of the kingdom, we must return to it to discern the larger work that God is doing there. And then we must continually return to the assembly of God's people with new data, new hypotheses, new proposals: "I thought I felt his presence in the consciousness-raising group the other evening." "I sensed his guidance in the meeting of the black caucus." "I think the Lord was speaking to me through a film shown at the meeting of the Rotary Club." "What do you think about these things, people of God? Let us attempt to prove what is good and acceptable and perfect, so that we can be transformed by the renewing of our minds."

6

Good News for the Poor

IN RECENT YEARS, the Christian community has given renewed attention to what the Bible has to say about poverty. This increased attention has resulted, to some degree, from the emergence of "liberation theology," but this is not the only factor. Many Third World Christians have become vocal critics of a white Western Christianity that has often ignored what the Bible says about poverty. And the news media have from time to time given extensive coverage to areas of the world in which hunger and malnutrition are critical problems. Black and Hispanic theologians in North America have insisted that the churches give an account of their relationships to the centers of financial and political power.

Theological reflection about the plight of the poor has not always filtered down to the people who sit in the pews. This is regrettable. The insistence that a concern for the poor and the oppressed of the earth is a central feature of the Christian gospel is not in all likelihood—nor ought it to be—a passing theological fad. It is my own conviction that this is such a central biblical concern that we cannot discuss the nature and calling of the laity without asking how the mission of the people of God relates to the situation of the oppressed. In the next chapter we will discuss some of the practical dimensions of this question; but we must first look at how this theme is treated in the biblical setting.

The Biblical Types

The Bible portrays God as having a very special concern for the poor and oppressed. In the Old Testament this concern is directed

toward the plights of certain social *types*. Psalm 146 provides a rather
detailed list of these types: God is described as one

> who executes justice for the oppressed;
> who gives food to the hungry.

> The Lord sets the prisoners free;
> the Lord opens the eyes of the blind.
> The Lord lifts up those who are bowed down;
> the Lord loves the righteous.
> The Lord watches over the sojourners,
> he upholds the widow and the fatherless;
> but the way of the wicked he brings to ruin.
>
>   (vv. 7–9)

The various types of persons mentioned have something in common. The underlying pattern exemplified by this list is especially
obvious in the case of the widow and the orphan. In a strongly
patriarchal social system, such as we find in the Old Testament,
power is possessed primarily by the adult male. Other persons have
access to the legal, political, and economic system only insofar as
they have adult males to represent their cause. In such a system the
widow and the orphan lack power: the widow is husbandless; the
orphan is fatherless. Both have no adult male to take up their cause.
Widows and orphans are helpless before the legal, political, and
economic structures of society.

Over and over again in the Old Testament special concern is shown
for the widow and the orphan. They have no human defenders to
speak out on their behalf, so God himself becomes their defender:
"Father of the fatherless and protector of widows is God in his holy
habitation" (Ps. 68:5). It should also be noted that this is one of those
biblical situations in which it would destroy the impact of the message
to eliminate references to the "masculinity" of God. Here God is
functioning as the *supreme* Father and Husband. He possesses in-
finitely more power than ordinary fathers and husbands, and he has
chosen to exercise that power on behalf of those who have failed to
gain the attention of human males.

The other types of persons mentioned in the Psalmist's list have
similar plights of legal, political, and economic helplessness. The
sojourner or "stranger" is either passing through the land on travels
or is living there as a slave or a temporary resident. He or she lacks the

rights of citizenship and experiences the psychological powerlessness of being unfamiliar with the language and customs.

Although it is difficult to ascertain precisely what is meant by the reference to prisoners, it is clear that the Bible offers liberation at least to those who have been unjustly imprisoned or taken captive. But the biblical call to justice goes further than this: it includes a concern for those criminals whose punishment exceeds their crimes. In systems where there are no proper legal safeguards, prisoners are often deprived of human rights; they are left to rot in their cells, their pleas for mercy going unheeded. It is quite possible that the reference to "the blind" whose eyes will be opened by the Lord is a mere repetition of the prisoner theme: some scholars think that this is another way of referring to persons who have been imprisoned in dark cells for so long that they are virtually blind.

The "oppressed" and those "who are bowed down" seem to be persons suffering under political tyranny. The reference to the "hungry" has to do with those persons who are at the mercy of others for their basic sustenance.

There is, then, a unity among the types mentioned in Psalm 146. Each is a type of person who, for one reason or another, is helpless before the structures of society. Each is legally "voiceless" and defenseless. In each case there is no one who *must* hear the pleadings of the person in question. And it is to such pleadings that the God of Israel inclines his ear. He takes up the cause of those who have no advocate. He has chosen to become the Defender of the defenseless.

The Appeal to the Powerful

What *happens* when God takes up the cause of the helpless ones? It is not as if God's concern is expedited in such a way that the structures of society will be left untouched. God does not say to the powerful of Israel: "You go about your business as usual. I'll look out for the concerns of the widow, the orphan, the sojourner, and the prisoner." No, God takes up their cause by calling their plight to the attention of the powerful.

This pattern of divine advocacy is obvious in the "legislative" writings of the Old Testament. Here are two of many such cases:

> You shall not wrong a stranger or oppress him, for you were strangers in the land of Egypt. You shall not afflict any widow or orphan. If you do

afflict them, and they cry out to me, I will surely hear their cry; and my wrath will burn, and I will kill you with the sword, and your wives shall become widows and your children fatherless.

(Ex. 22:21–24)

He [God] executes justice for the fatherless and the widow, and loves the sojourner, giving him food and clothing. Love the sojourner therefore; for you were sojourners in the land of Egypt.

(Deut. 10:18–19)

These two examples (and many others in the Old Testament) exhibit a common theme. Israel must attend to the needs of the widow, the orphan, and the sojourner because "you were strangers in the land of Egypt." The appeal here is to Israel's own past. When Israel was held in slavery in Egypt, she was utterly helpless. She cried out to her oppressors for mercy, but the oppressors turned a deaf ear. But *God* heard Israel's cry. And even though Israel had no "rights" before God, no special "standing" in his eyes, he heard the cries of the oppressed, took up the cause of the weak, and delivered Israel from the yoke of bondage. And now he admonishes Israel: "You were once weak and helpless before me, and I became your defender. Now you in turn must hear the cries of the helpless ones and go to their aid, or you will become strangers to me again."

This note of judgment on those who are oblivious to the concerns of the helpless is especially strong in the prophetic writings of the Old Testament:

Woe to those who decree iniquitous decrees,
and the writers who keep writing oppression,
to turn aside the needy from justice
and to rob the poor of my people of their right,
that widows may be their spoil,
and that they may make the fatherless their prey!
What will you do on the day of punishment,
in the storm which will come from afar?
To whom will you flee for help,
and where will you leave your wealth?

(Isa. 10:1–3)

Here we find the same theme: if those who have power despise the cause of the needy, they will someday find themselves powerless, with nowhere to turn.

The Lazy Poor

Those who read the Old Testament with an eye to these matters will find that the summary of the case that we have presented thus far points to matters that show up with great frequency there. But they will also find another pattern of thought. In the Old Testament, and especially in what is called the Wisdom literature, the poor are sometimes referred to in disparaging ways. Here is an example:

> How long will you lie there, O sluggard?
> When will you arise from your sleep?
> A little sleep, a little slumber,
> a little folding of the hands to rest,
> and poverty will come upon you like a vagabond,
> and want like an armed man.
>
> (Prov. 6:9–11)

Here poverty is viewed as something that comes upon a person because of laziness, a theme repeated in Proverbs 10:4: "A slack hand causes poverty, but the hand of the diligent makes rich."

Is there a contradiction between this perspective and the expressions of concern for the widow, orphan, sojourner, and prisoner? Are there two conflicting biblical analyses of poverty? There is no reason to think so. What we have here are two dimensions of a larger picture, two strands in the overall biblical perspective on poverty. The observations in the book of Proverbs about the relationship between sloth and poverty have to do, as Julio de Santa Ana points out, with "the exhortation to work and a serious and earnest approach to life" (*Good News to the Poor,* page 1).

The Bible views work as a very serious matter. In the first creation account in Genesis the human pair was given a mandate by the Creator to "fill the earth and subdue it; and have dominion . . ." (Gen. 1:28). Human beings were created to be active laborers in the good creation. We might put it this way: we are intended by God to fulfill ourselves through meaningful labor. Work is not, of course, the *whole* of human life; we must take seriously the cycles of work, play, and rest. But work is an important expression of the kind of nature we possess.

The rebellion of Adam and Eve brought a curse on the process of work; human interaction with nature was from that point on to be a task characterized by toil and sweat. But God's redemptive dealings with the human race have made it possible once again for labor to be carried on out of a desire to serve God and our neighbors.

Therefore, for those who are capable of labor to refuse to engage in it is taken to be a sign of rebellion. Laziness is viewed in the Bible as willful rebellion against God and a failure to act responsibly toward our fellow human beings. The slothful person, then, will not be allowed to escape the consequences of his or her irresponsibility.

Of course, there are important discussions taking place today about the place of work in a society in which time for leisure activity has greatly increased. Christians must take these discussions seriously, with a clear recognition of the social forces that have influenced contemporary attitudes toward work and leisure. Indeed, these matters call for creative thinking on the part of the Christian community. But that thinking must also take into account the biblical admonitions against irresponsible idleness.

In the biblical context, however, these admonitions do not apply to the widow, the orphan, and the other types mentioned in Psalm 146. They are not being willfully lazy. They are not guilty of sloth and rebellion. They are being prohibited from entering into patterns of responsible labor. They have no proper place in the world of bargaining and decision-making. They are being prevented by the very structures of society from acting as responsible agents in the good creation. To such persons, God becomes not a Judge but a Defender.

Mary's Song

The Old Testament emphasis on God's concern for the powerless ones is not lost on the New Testament community. Here, too, God is viewed as the one who cares in a special way for those who are helpless before the structures of society.

Mary's song in Luke 1 is a good example of this emphasis:

My soul magnifies the Lord,
and my spirit rejoices in God my Savior,
for he has regarded the low estate of his handmaiden.
For behold, henceforth all generations will call me blessed;
for he who is mighty has done great things for me,
and holy is his name.
And his mercy is on those who fear him
from generation to generation.

He has shown strength with his arm,
he has scattered the proud in the imagination of their hearts,
he has put down the mighty from their thrones,
and exalted those of low degree;
he has filled the hungry with good things,
and the rich he has sent empty away.
He has helped his servant Israel,
in remembrance of his mercy,
as he spoke to our fathers,
to Abraham and to his posterity for ever.

                                                    (Luke 1:46–55)

It is important to understand these words against the background of
Mary's situation. She is a pregnant virgin, and she became pregnant
while being unmarried but betrothed to Joseph. Our earlier observations about patriarchal societies are relevant here. In a patriarchy,
when a young woman like Mary gets into a difficult situation it is
important that she have an adult male to defend her. But Mary is in a
kind of "no man's land." She is—as a betrothed woman—no longer
clearly under her father's care, but—as an unmarried woman—she is
not yet under Joseph's. Who will take up her case? Who will defend
her, especially when she has become pregnant in a manner she herself
cannot explain?

It was thus to a very vulnerable young woman that God sent the
angel Gabriel with a significant message: "Do not be afraid, Mary, for
you have found favor with God" (Luke 1:30). The God who is the
Defender of widows and orphans has also chosen to take up Mary's
cause. It is because of this joyous news that Mary can announce to
Elizabeth: "he has regarded the low estate of his handmaiden."

The word for "regarded" here can also be translated "noticed" or
"glanced at." We might think of the situation of a beggar who has
been sitting by the city gate for hours, crying out for alms. The crowd
hurries by, oblivious to his cries. Then suddenly someone glances in
his direction, stops, and reaches into a pocket for coins. The beggar's
heart leaps: "He noticed! Someone heard my pleadings!"

The same sense of wonder and jubilation is being expressed by
Mary. God noticed her helpless, powerless condition. No one *had* to
take up her cause. She could have been left standing helpless before
the structures—before authorities who would have been extremely
harsh and merciless toward her. But God intervened, taking on him-

self the role of her protector. "He noticed!" And the general implications of this fact are not lost on Mary. She quickly generalizes from her own case to speak of the political and economic designs of this God who has taken up her cause: he will scatter those who are proud, knocking the mighty from their thrones, lifting up the powerless ones; he will feed the hungry and send the rich away empty-handed.

Lest it be thought that we are reading too much into this passage, it is important to note that Jesus repeats the same themes, a few chapters later in Luke's Gospel account, in choosing what is often called his "inaugural text" at the synagogue in Nazareth. There, at the very beginning of his public ministry, he is asked to read from the prophecy of Isaiah. He chooses these words:

> The Spirit of the Lord is upon me,
> because he has anointed me to preach good news to the poor.
> He has sent me to proclaim release to the captives,
> and recovering of sight to the blind,
> to set at liberty those who are oppressed,
> to proclaim the acceptable year of the Lord.
>
> (Luke 4:18–19)

Women in the New Testament

Mary's song has to be understood against the background of the role of women in a patriarchal society. Like the widow and the orphan of the Old Testament, Mary becomes a special concern of God, as over against patterns of social interaction that restrict legal standing to the adult male. This is an important factor to recognize in current discussions of the role of women in church and society. When Christians talk about "what the Bible says about women," they often restrict the discussion to those passages, especially in the Pauline letters, in which the husband-wife relationship is being explicitly discussed.

Even in those "conservative"-sounding passages, of course, the focus of the contemporary reader is often on the wrong elements. It is not so surprising that in a male-dominated society the apostles—with their concern that Christians "be subject for the Lord's sake to every human institution"—should, as Paul does in Ephesians 5:22, advise wives to "be subject to your husbands, as to the Lord." What *is* surprising, though, is that he would in the preceding verse tell husbands and wives to "be subject *to one another* out of reverence for Christ," and that, a few verses later, in verse 25, he would tell husbands to love their wives "as Christ loved the church and gave himself up for her." Similarly, when Paul says, in 1 Corinthians 7:4, that in the matter of conjugal rights, "the husband does not rule over his own body, but the wife does," Paul is presenting a significant challenge to the sexual status quo.

The Bible, I believe, lays the groundwork for releasing women from the degrading and oppressive roles that have been imposed on them by patriarchal societies. Already in the Gospel accounts significant steps are taken to grant to women a standing and a "voice" that are denied them by the structures of social interaction. Three out of four evangelists record the fact that the women who were at the empty tomb were given an explicit command, either by an angel or by Jesus, to tell the male disciples about the resurrection. Once again women are "regarded" in a situation in which their testimony has no legal standing.

In Jewish society the testimony of women would not be accepted as evidence in legal proceedings. As witnesses, women lacked acceptable credibility. But at the empty tomb they were told to "tell the brethren" what they had seen and heard. Luke is the only writer who does not record this command. Instead, he informs us of the disciples' reaction to the women's story: "but these words seemed to them an idle tale, and they did not believe them" (Luke 24:11).

The disciples were wrong not to realize that even here God was noticing the low estate of his handmaidens. Later one of these disciples would make a special point of telling husbands in the early church to offer "honor" to their wives "as the weaker sex"—an explicit recognition of the facts of legal, economic, and political life—"since you are joint heirs of the grace of life, in order that your prayers may not be hindered" (1 Pet. 3:7–8). Peter has learned here the lesson of Easter morning as it applies to the role of women. And the lesson is consistent with the Psalmist's insistence that God hears the cries of the helpless ones. God takes the words of women seriously, and so the male members of the Christian community must do so as well. If they refuse to do so, their own prayers will be "hindered." God will not listen to those who are in turn oblivious to the cries of the powerless.

Mary had learned that lesson much earlier. She saw the important implications of what God was doing in committing himself to her seemingly helpless cause. She would not have been surprised to hear the words that her son would speak to another Mary: "Go and tell my brethren." The mother of Jesus knew, early on in the process, what the disciples were to learn only through bitter humiliation: that never again should the words of women be treated as "an idle tale." The Apostles began to introduce the necessary correctives into the life of the family and the church, patterns that—or so it seems to me—must continue to be revised and expanded in the life of the people of God today.

The Poor in Spirit

I once heard a black speaker gently chide his white Christian audience for reading the Bible from the perspective of a "honky hermeneutic." Our "hermeneutic" has to do with the way in which we interpret the Scriptures. This speaker was suggesting that the Bible is often read from a white middle-class perspective, especially when dealing with biblical passages about poverty.

One thing we have often done is to latch onto any verse in the Bible that will reinforce our own prejudices and our own positions of privilege. For example, I have discovered that in speaking to white middle-class audiences about the biblical perspective on poverty, it is almost a certainty that someone will quote Jesus' statement to the disciples: "For you always have the poor with you, but you will not always have me" (Matt. 26:11; see also Mark 14:7 and John 12:8).

When this statement is quoted, it is often brought up in order to detract from the case being made, that the Bible demonstrates a central concern on God's part for the poor. But, of course, this statement cannot be legitimately used for that purpose. Jesus is not commanding his disciples to ignore the needs of the poor; he is not saying, "Make sure that there are always poor people around!" He is defending the gesture of a woman who had anointed Jesus with a very expensive jar of perfume. He is commending her for recognizing his unique presence. It is not that a concern for the poor is a bad thing. But neither is it a bad thing that this woman brings a special gift to Jesus.

Another way in which people often try to blunt the biblical message

regarding poverty is by "spiritualizing" many of the biblical references to the poor. An important verse for these purposes is Matthew
5:3, one of the "beatitudes": "Blessed are the poor in spirit, for theirs
is the kingdom of heaven." Here Jesus links being "poor" with a
certain kind of spiritual condition; blessedness is promised to those
who experience "spiritual poverty." Once this kind of case has been
made, some people seem to find it quite natural to read "poor in
spirit" into every reference to "the poor." For example, Jesus' use of
the Isaiah passage as his inaugural text in Luke 4 can then be read
along these lines: The Spirit of the Lord is upon me . . . to preach good
news to the poor *in spirit*.

Once the "honky hermeneutic" gets us this far, it seems to be clear
sailing from here on in. For aren't all of us as Christians—bankers,
suburban homemakers, grocery store clerks, corporate managers,
salespersons, clergy—"poor in spirit"? The main thing to cultivate in
order to achieve this kind of spiritual poverty is to be humble, to be
aware of our dependence on God, to experience those troubled mo-
ments when we despair over our own sinfulness.

But this line of argument will not do. A glance at a concordance of
the Bible will demonstrate that there are hundreds of places in the
Bible where the "poor" are mentioned. Over and over again these
references indicate that God has a very special concern for those who
are economically and politically deprived. There is simply no way in
which these numerous instances can be understood as referring to a
pattern of "spiritual poverty."

There is something strange going on when Christian people focus
exclusively on a dozen or so biblical verses that can be "spiri-
tualized" when constructing their own understanding of poverty,
thereby ignoring the hundreds of places where the Bible makes it
absolutely clear that God is very much concerned about those who
are victims of economic, political, and legal injustice. Given the
overall biblical message, we must interpret the "spiritualizing" passages in the light of the numerous verses that deal with the hard
economic facts rather than the other way around.

It is interesting that the "beatitude" found in Matthew 5:3 is given a
somewhat different formulation in Luke 6:20: "Blessed are you poor,
for yours is the kingdom of God." Here the "in spirit" qualification is
not present; the reference is more clearly economic in nature. It

seems to be the case that these two formulations complement each other. With all its references to poverty, the Bible never romanticizes the condition of being poor. The "blessedness" experienced by those who are helpless before the structures of society does not result from the fact that being politically and economically deprived is intrinsically enjoyable.

We might put the case this way: the Bible does not teach that poverty is either a necessary or a sufficient condition for experiencing the blessedness of the kingdom of God. It is not necessary, because there is no absolute requirement that we become economically deprived in order to be acceptable to God. And it is not sufficient, in that being or becoming economically deprived does not give us automatic entrance into the kingdom. What then *is* the relationship between being poor and experiencing the blessedness of the kingdom? The answer seems to be found along these lines. In order to enter into the kingdom of God, we must recognize our own utter helplessness. We must realize that divine grace is a free gift, a gift that we cannot in any way earn by means of our own efforts. The blessedness of the kingdom is found by throwing ourselves completely on the mercy of God.

In short, we can experience the peace of the kingdom of Jesus only if we have come to see that all our own "props" are of no avail to us. We must experience "prop-less-ness." But many of us have a difficult time arriving at this awareness. We are accustomed to "making it" on our own. We are inclined to rely on our jobs, or on status, or on our sense of self-worth. In that sense, it is much easier for the poor—the widow, the orphan, the sojourner, and so on—to gain entrance into the kingdom. They do not have the "props" the rest of us are accustomed to relying on. They know their own utter helplessness. This seems to be what is being said when Jesus observes that "it will be hard for a rich man to enter the kingdom of heaven" (Matt. 19:23)—not impossible, note, but "hard."

It is not absolutely necessary, then, to be literally "poor" in order to enter the kingdom; what is required is that we be "poor in spirit." But the utter helplessness associated with economic poverty is closely associated with spiritual poverty. Those of us who are privileged in an economic and political sense will have a much more difficult time casting aside all the "props" that serve as hindrances to entering the kingdom.

The Promise of Abundance

But we must stress the point once again that the Scriptures do not romanticize poverty. Poverty is an evil condition. It is something God hates. Human beings are created for the purpose of enjoying the riches of the good creation. Poverty is incompatible with—indeed, it is a violation of—God's creating and redeeming purposes. Of course, even this evil condition has, in a sense, a good side to it: those who experience it are aware of their own utter helplessness, which is an important prerequisite for entrance into the kingdom. But God does not desire that anyone remain in a condition of poverty. For all who have cast their cares on him, he has promised the abundant life.

This does not mean, however, that those of us who presently experience economic privilege can simply view our situation as one of divine favor. God wants all his children to live in abundance. But as long as some of his children are experiencing the desperation of poverty, all of us are called to cast our lot with them. As long as economic and political helplessness exist, we must count the promise of abundant living to be just that—a promise. And if that promise is delayed for some, it must be delayed for all of us who yearn for the appearance of the fullness of the kingdom.

This pattern of living with a yearning for a kingdom that is not yet fully visible is a difficult one. It raises many questions about the appropriate economic and political attitudes for the people of God in today's world. We must now turn to some of the practical dimensions of these questions.

7

Identifying with the Poor: More Questions

ONCE AGAIN we must acknowledge the gap that exists between the ancient world of the Bible and our own times. The Bible was written to, and by, persons who lived in very different cultures from our present social environment. The Bible is also, of course, the authoritative vehicle for God's revelation to his people today. The Spirit of God makes this ancient record come alive for us, so that words written long ago can function for us as a living and contemporary guide for faith and practice.

But this does not mean that we can simply apply the Bible to the contemporary world in a mechanical fashion. We must work hard to interpret the biblical message correctly, seeking proper points of contact between its original intentions and the situations in which we presently find ourselves. It is important to keep this in mind as we attempt to live in obedience to what the Bible says about the poor. It will certainly not do simply to take every biblical reference to "the poor" and treat it as if it applied automatically to the condition of those who are *called* "the poor" today.

Our discussion in the previous chapter of the biblical message regarding the poor was hardly an exhaustive treatment of the subject. But we did say enough on the subject to point to some crucial areas of practical concern for the people of God in the twentieth century. By returning here to the question-and-answer format, we can expand on some of those concerns, as well as exploring further the scope and intentions of the biblical message for this topic.

When the biblical writers talk about the poor, aren't they talking about the "saved" poor?

There is something to be said in favor of this suggestion. Much of what is said about the poor in the Old Testament refers to the poor of Israel. It is also possible that, when Jesus spoke about "good news to the poor," he was thinking primarily of the poor of Palestine. And the apostolic references to "orphans and widows" may well be references to poor persons who are a part of the Christian community.

But the Old Testament's concern for the poor is not expressed exclusively on behalf of the poor "of the house of Israel." The concern for the "stranger" and the "sojourner," for example, is meant to prod the Israelites into thinking beyond the confines of their own ethnic group. Similarly, when Amos criticizes the injustice inflicted on the poor within Israel, he goes on to criticize the unjust patterns of Israel's pagan neighbors. There is a strong suggestion in the Old Testament that the heart of God goes out to the cries of the oppressed, regardless of where those oppressed persons are living.

The patterns of caring for the poor in the New Testament church do seem to focus primarily on the poor of the church. This seems clear, for example, in the book of Acts. But once again, this is not the exclusive emphasis. The Epistle of James places great stress on a concern for the poor, and many of the comments there are focused on the ways in which the poor are treated within the life of the church: he warns church members, for example, not to favor the rich with the good seats in the assembly of Christians while the poor members are shunted aside (James 2:1–7). But James also speaks to the "systemic" issue of how the poor are treated in the larger (pagan) society:

> Come now, you rich, weep and howl for the miseries that are coming upon you. Your riches have rotted and your garments are moth-eaten. Your gold and silver have rusted, and their rust will be evidence against you and will eat your flesh like fire. You have laid up treasure for the last days. Behold, the wages of the laborers who mowed your fields, which you kept back by fraud, cry out; and the cries of the harvesters have reached the ears of the Lord of hosts.
>
> (James 5:1–4)

Romans 12 is another case in point. Verses 9 through 21 are a series of practical instructions to the church, which can be divided into two sections, following my earlier distinction between "domestic" and "foreign" policy. The first section seems to be primarily concerned with the "internal" life of the Christian community:

> Let love be genuine; hate what is evil, hold fast to what is good; love one another with brotherly affection; outdo one another in showing honor.

Never flag in zeal, be aglow with the Spirit, serve the Lord. Rejoice in your hope, be patient in tribulation, be constant in prayer. Contribute to the needs of the saints, practice hospitality.

(Rom. 12:9–13)

The instructions here seem to bear, in good part, on how Christians ought to treat one another. But the second section includes much that has to do with the ways in which Christians relate to the larger human community:

Bless those who persecute you; bless and do not curse them. Rejoice with those who rejoice, weep with those who weep. Live in harmony with one another; do not be haughty, but associate with the lowly; never be conceited. Repay no one evil for evil, but take thought of what is noble in the sight of all. If possible, so far as it depends upon you, live peaceably with all. Beloved, never avenge yourselves, but leave it to the wrath of God; for it is written, "Vengeance is mine, I will repay, says the Lord." No, "if your enemy is hungry, feed him; if he is thirsty, give him drink; for by so doing you will heap burning coals upon his head." Do not be overcome by evil, but overcome evil with good.

(Rom. 12:14–21)

There are important parallels between these instructions and the language of 1 Peter 2, discussed at length earlier—for example, Peter's "honor all men" and Paul's "live peaceably with all"; and Peter's "love the brotherhood" and Paul's "love one another with brotherly affection." These instructions in Romans 12 may well be taken as a specification of the "good works" and "good conduct" of 1 Peter 2 and Romans 13.

What is most important for our present consideration is the fact that Paul, in this Romans 12 passage, speaks of the need to be concerned for the poor both within the church and in the larger society: "contribute to the needs of the saints"; "associate with the lowly"; "if your enemy is hungry, feed him." I once heard a story about a pastoral counselor who was talking with a man who was bound and determined to divorce his wife. The counselor asked him how he reconciled his position with the biblical mandate for husbands to love their wives. The man quickly replied, "After what she's done, I don't consider her to be my wife any more!" "Well, then," the counselor replied, "she is still your neighbor, and the Bible says that we must love our neighbors." After a moment's pause, the man replied, "I guess I don't really think that she's even my neighbor any more!" To which the counselor responded: "Well, then, you had better get serious about loving your enemy!"

There is a similar pattern of biblical teaching that applies to the Christian obligation to show concern for the poor. At the very least we must identify with the needs of those poor persons who are our fellow Christians. But even where that obligation fails to apply, there is still the need to serve those poor who are simply our neighbors. And if anyone thinks that this obligation is in some sense a restrictive one, the Apostle pushes the boundaries out even further: "If your enemy is hungry, feed him."

But I must also express my conviction that, even if some Christians want to limit their obligations to those poor persons who are fellow Christians, that is still a very significant commitment. There are millions of Christians in Latin America and Asia whose physical and economic situation is desperate; and there are millions of Christian brothers and sisters in South Africa and elsewhere who suffer under the yoke of oppression. If there are some affluent Christians who, because of theological scruples, want to limit their efforts to expressing genuine solidarity with those Christian persons, they will not find themselves lacking in significant moral and economic and political commitments.

Mustn't Christians be careful to distinguish between the "deserving" and the "undeserving" poor?

Of course. A concern for the poor must be coordinated with at least two other concerns the Christian community ought to take seriously. The first is a desire on our part not to foster laziness and dependence. In outlining biblical attitudes toward the poor, I noted that the Old Testament includes warnings and condemnations regarding those who become poor because of their deliberate refusal to work. It is not good for people to be reinforced in their sloth, nor is it proper for Christians to encourage people to become dependent on charity when they are capable of providing for their own livelihood.

The second concern is closely related to the first: the desire to be good stewards over the resources we have received. This means that we must be very responsible and attentive in giving to the poor. There is a real danger among affluent Christians that they will engage in acts of charity primarily out of a desire to assuage their own feelings of guilt. We have an obligation not only to share what we have, but to share in such a way that what we are giving gets into the hands of those who are genuinely needy.

But, of course, none of this is meant to excuse us from making the necessary sacrifices. It is especially not meant as a basis for refusing to take risks. It certainly seems better to take a chance that something might end up in the hands of the undeserving poor than to do nothing at all. Strictly speaking, of course, we are all "undeserving" of what we have. So we must not apply this concept too strictly, as seems to be pointed out in several of Jesus' parables.

It is not the worst sin to have given something, out of a sincere desire to be obedient to the gospel, that somehow gets into the hands of an undeserving person. A desire to be careful stewards, then, must be coupled with a willingness to take risks and to be flexible in our attitudes toward the poor.

There are even distinctions that must be made *within* the category of the "deserving" poor. Some poor or deprived persons have problems that make "rehabilitation" difficult or impossible—e.g., the elderly or persons who are severely handicapped, physically or mentally. Others need, not long-range charity, but the kind of assistance that leads to nondependence. It is important, then, to be sure that we are not offering dependence-producing charity where other kinds of assistance—including the support that comes through attempts at structural change—are required.

Some of your comments about "work" sound like a replay of the old "Protestant ethic." Is that what you intend?

I think that the so-called Protestant work ethic has often received a bad press it does not deserve. The important thing is to get clear about what is demanded by a biblical perspective on work and leisure. If that perspective in the final analysis approximates the Protestant work ethic, so be it; if not, so much for the Protestant work ethic.

Karl Marx insisted that we somehow fulfill our deepest impulses as human beings when we engage in labor. A human being looks at a rough log lying in the forest and imagines the way in which that log could be transformed into a table. Then he sets to work and transforms that rough wood into the table he has envisioned. For Marx, he has "objectified" himself in that act; he has taken a private, subjective plan and made it a part of the public world by transforming nature into the works of his own hands.

Whenever I teach my students that part of Marx's philosophical perspective, I am impressed by how closely it approximates the "feel" of the creation stories in Genesis 1 and 2. God creates the first human pair to interact with nature, bringing the natural realm into subjection to the will of the Creator as it is mediated through human beings, who are charged by God to "have dominion" over the nonhuman creation. Human beings were created to tend the garden, to bring out, in a loving, caring manner, the "best" in the creation.

This does not mean that we were created *only* to engage in communal labor. There is also a larger cycle of activities, of which work is only a part, that includes play, worship, celebrating the "flesh of my flesh" relationships, and so on. But work—meaningful labor in the context of the good earth—is a crucial element in all of this.

That is how, as I see it, we must interpret those biblical passages that condemn laziness. It is simply not good for human beings to live lives of consistent leisure or to be condemned to a pattern of total dependence on the labors of other persons. Consequently, it seems to me that Christians must be very much concerned about patterns of unemployment that virtually guarantee that groups of persons who are capable of engaging in meaningful work are deprived of that involvement.

Doesn't a consideration of the Christian's obligation to the poor ultimately lead us to think about economic systems?

I recently heard a Third World Christian comment that in the past the question was "How can a Christian be a socialist?" while now it is "How can a Christian be a capitalist?" It certainly is the case that more and more Christians these days are thinking about what sort of economic *system* we ought to be advocating.

I myself am not prepared to offer a wholesale condemnation of capitalism as such, and I can't say that I find ideological socialism compelling. My main concern in this area has to do with the ways in which Christians and others often express their economic convictions. For example, one way of defending capitalism is on the kinds of "social Darwinist" grounds popular in the late nineteenth century—a perspective that has a lingering influence today. In this perspective, the economic arena operates best after the manner of "the law of the jungle." Economic life is a testing ground to see who will survive. In a completely open, competitive situation, we can be certain that the "fit" will survive and the "unfit" will sink to the bottom of the economic heap.

There are a number of very common clichés associated with this outlook: "You get what you work for"; "God helps those who help themselves"; "If you don't work, you don't eat." And there is a general assumption operating in this viewpoint that those who succeed economically deserve to succeed, while those who fail deserve to fail.

However we come out ultimately on the merits of a free-market system, *this* pattern of defending such a system is unacceptable from a Christian perspective. There are many persons who fail to "succeed" economically, not because of any basic character defect on their part, but because of structural injustice. Because of biases against various racial groups, the handicapped, women, and others, it is unfair to view the economic arena as a place in which all of us start with the same opportunities. The Bible is very clear in pointing to various groups that are at a serious disadvantage in this area—thus our discussion of the widow, the orphan, the sojourner, and the like. The biblical writers are not afraid to condemn societies in which various groups are locked out of the patterns of full economic participation, nor are they reluctant to criticize the wealthy for perpetuating injustice through greed and unfair competition.

I have a special concern in this area that stems from my own commitment to Calvinist doctrine. I view the Bible as basically teaching a "handout" view of salvation. We do not deserve God's grace. God's gift of his son as a payment for sin was a pure act of divine mercy. This theme permeates much Protestant piety. Take, for example, the "handout" tone of many evangelical hymns and songs: "Nothing in my hands I bring, simply to the cross I cling"; "Nought have I gotten but what I've received"; "Not what these hands have done, can save my guilty soul."

It strikes me as odd that many of us can give sincere expression to this kind of piety, in which economic *metaphors* play a dominant role, and yet can turn around to promote a thoroughgoing "works-righteousness" in the economic sphere. The biblical writers do not follow our pattern of treating salvation and economics in two very different ways. In both areas all of us are undeserving. In both areas what we receive is to be viewed as a gift of divine grace. And, just as God has heard the cries for mercy that we have uttered in our spiritual helplessness, so we are to hear the cries for mercy of those who are economically helpless.

Once again: I don't know if this means that we must be critical of capitalism as such. But it certainly means that we have to be critical of many attitudes that are associated with energetic *defenses* of capitalist systems.

How come we're hearing so much more lately in Christian circles about the Bible's emphasis on the poor?

Ours is not the first generation to notice that God has a very central and extensive regard for the poor and the oppressed. A sense that the Christian community must make a radical commitment to the poor is to be found in the traditions of every branch of Christendom: Roman Catholicism, Eastern Orthodoxy, Lutheranism, the Anabaptist tradition, Reformed Christianity, Wesleyanism, Anglicanism, the Baptist churches, European pietism.

The way in which this emphasis has been spelled out in the past, especially in Eastern Orthodoxy and Roman Catholicism, is outlined helpfully in Julio de Santa Ana's book *Good News to the Poor: The Challenge of the Poor in the History of the Church.* Other helpful discussions can be found in studies of the lives and teachings of John Calvin, John Wesley, St. Francis of Assisi, Menno Simons, and other historical figures.

When I am talking about this subject to persons of my own Reformed tradition, I find it helpful to quote John Calvin. One of Calvin's favorite arguments against the Roman Catholic hierarchy was that they had become unfaithful to their own traditions of identifying in a radical way with the concerns of the poor. Calvin tells church leaders that they ought to melt all their gold fixtures and ornaments and use the gold to ransom prisoners, and he complains that Christians take the money that should be given to the poor and use it in "constructing churches, erecting statues, buying vessels, and providing sacred vestments. Thus are daily alms consumed in this abyss"

(*Institutes of the Christian Religion,* Book IV, Chapter V). It seems clear that Calvin would be very critical of the present-day habits of many of his ecclesiastical descendants!

The recent emphasis on the "theology of the poor" is not a new invention. It is the discovery of an ancient and precious tradition to be found in all branches of the Christian church. The important question, then, is: How did we wander so far away from the radical visions of our own theological and church traditions?

Is the Christian gospel exclusively "good news for the poor"? Isn't there a word of hope for affluent persons as well?

The pastor of a suburban church recently asked me this question in a rather poignant fashion: "The more I study the Scriptures, the more I am convinced that the gospel is a message of joyous good news for the poor. But I have no poor people in my congregation; all my parishioners are quite affluent. In what sense can I preach *good* news to the affluent people of the suburbs? What bothers me most is the fact that most of my parishioners are quite content with their luxurious patterns of living—they don't want to be reminded of their obligations to the less fortunate. Don't I have to preach judgment to them? Or is there a way in which I can preach good news to them as well?"

This is an important line of questioning, for which I cannot provide definitive answers. As a beginning, however, it seems clear that if everything we have said thus far is true, there is something very wrong about the attitudes and lives of church members who want to pursue affluent life-styles without having to be bothered by reminders of their obligations to the poor. In a very basic sense, the message of good news to them must be a conditional one: there is good news for them only *if* they are willing to repent of their sins and turn to the way of committed Christian discipleship.

Assuming that this is the proper way of viewing things, how is this pastor—who seems quite sensitive to the realities of the situation—to pursue a ministry in their midst? Indeed, how are all of us, clergy and laity alike, who are concerned about these matters, to pursue ministries among the affluent?

To begin with, we must want the affluent to change their attitudes, to come to a point in their spiritual pilgrimages where they understand that the heart of God goes out in a special way to the widow, the orphan, the beggar, and the sojourner and that God desperately wants these church members to share that concern. This is the foundation for a proper pastoral approach to them.

But we must also be sure that our own pride and anger do not get in the way of a genuine pastoral approach to such persons. We must be certain that our message to them is not motivated by a desire to "be radical." The important thing is for these persons to hear, not the anger of self-righteous Christians, but the pleas of a loving God being conveyed from the lips of fellow sinners.

Ministries among the affluent have an important educational dimension. We must attempt to bring affluent church members into a fuller understanding of the gospel, with a genuine sensitivity to "where they are at" presently. It may even be necessary to explore the ways in which the gospel *can* presently function as "good news" to them, even when they are still insensitive to the "good news for the poor."

For example, the pastor who addressed the question to me seemed to be describing persons who were proud and materialistic. But it is unlikely that this is the whole story. Affluent suburban homes are touched by many problems: grief, alcoholism, tensions between parents and children, marital instability, feelings of personal inadequacy. It may be necessary to approach such persons at their own points of vulnerability and "prop-less-ness." It may be necessary for them to experience God's gracious approach to them in their own unique experiences of helplessness before they are ready to share in God's concern for the economically and politically helpless.

The complexities of this problem are obvious from the way in which Jesus approached the rich and the powerful. Sometimes Jesus was very "judgmental." He wasted little time in making the demands of the gospel clear to the rich young ruler. And his approach to the Pharisees was often very direct and confrontational. In the case of Zacchaeus, however, he seems to have been very "pastoral." Zacchaeus apparently had a reputation as an oppressor of the poor. Yet Jesus was able to discern a sense of vulnerability in him. So he begins by reaching out in friendship to Zacchaeus, although it is clear that his goal is to bring Zacchaeus to the point where he repents of his sin and repairs his ways.

Are there perhaps varieties of "oppression," so that we might think of affluent suburbanites as also being "oppressed" or even "poor" in some sense?

I am inclined to think that there *are* varieties of "oppression." I remember a young black woman's telling me about a conference she had attended. Both blacks and white women were present, but the conference was dominated by white males. At one point both the women and the blacks decided to caucus. This young woman had to decide which caucus she would attend. With which group did she have most in common as a black woman: white women or black males? She put the dilemma in this way: "I had to decide which of my 'oppressions' was the greater—my oppression as a woman or my oppression as a black." She attended the black caucus.

This young woman distinguished between two kinds of oppression she had experienced, with regard to two different social roles. In her case, she decided that the racial oppression was greater than the oppression of sexism. But to admit that women, *as women,* experience oppression is to suggest that oppression is experienced among affluent suburbanites, since white suburbanite women have been discriminated against in the job market and elsewhere. But aren't there also other kinds of "oppression" experienced in the suburbs— for example, by children who are helpless before the rage of their parents, by a wife or husband who is victimized by a philandering spouse, by a stockbroker who is hanging on for dear life in a struggle against alcoholism, by those who are victimized by gossips and rumormongers, and so on?

My own inclination is to view "oppression" as something that occurs on a continuum, with, say, the black slave on one end and the millionaire's wife who is the object of unfounded, malicious rumors on the other. But I have black friends who balk at this view of things. They deny that the utter helplessness of the black slave can be put under the same conceptual umbrella as the rather paltry problems of the millionaire's wife.

I can sympathize with the spirit of this kind of resistance. But nonetheless there seem to me to be good "pastoral" reasons for the continuum picture. Earlier we noted that in the Old Testament God pleaded on behalf of the widow and the orphan by reminding the powerful Israelites that they were once helpless victims in the land of Egypt. There seem to me to be good arguments in favor of a similar pattern of argument today: "Do you remember what it was like to be helpless before those gossips, or before the temptation to drink? Do you remember what it was like to throw yourself upon the mercy of God? Well, you must reach out to those who have no one to turn to in their poverty, or in their political helplessness. . . ." It may be that these experiences, on the part of those who are normally reckoned to be rich and powerful, can open them to the full implications of the good news proclaimed in the Scriptures.

It is depressing to think about the problems of the poor. What can we do about them? Where do we even start?

I have no easy solutions to the problems of poverty and political oppression. I don't even have *difficult* solutions. But it is not difficult to think of places where each of us can begin to address the issues in significant ways.

First of all, we can pray. Prayer is a significant form of action. It is even a significant form of *political* action. Prayer is petitioning the King of the universe. To pray on behalf of the poor and oppressed, then, is to place their concerns before the very highest of authorities. It is *doing* something.

But if we are going to pray on behalf of the poor, we must pray intelligently. We must prepare ourselves for *informed* prayer. This means that we must study—read books, attend conferences, subscribe to magazines that deal with issues in this area. I stress these matters because of a genuine danger I see being posed by an "antiintellectual" streak that shows up in this area of concern. Christians are sometimes affected, to their detriment, by a pragmatic, activist mentality that shuns serious study. When it comes to dealing with the poor, however, it is extremely important that we engage in informed action. We owe this to those who are victims of economic oppression. Their plight is too serious for them to become the objects of concern on the part of people who operate with romantic or idealistic notions that are not disciplined by study of, and reflection on, the meaning and realities of economic and political suffering.

Another way to become informed is to get acquainted, on a firsthand basis, with the poverty that exists closest to us. We can ride or walk frequently in certain urban or rural pockets of poverty, familiarizing ourselves with the landscape of oppression, so that our prayers and sighs relate to flesh-and-blood scenarios. And we can seek out communities of concerned persons. We can draw on the resources of Christians who are already involved in these problems. We can establish discussion groups among friends and fellow Christians.

An important element here is the need for many of us to *listen* to the poor. Dialogue can be established with churches in poverty areas. Book clubs and church groups can read and discuss the literature of poverty.

We can make the concerns of the poor and oppressed central to our patterns of spirituality. Ronald Sider, in his excellent book *Rich Christians in a Hungry World,* outlines a proposal for a "graduated tithe," a helpful program for Christians who genuinely want to commit themselves to sacrificial living. There is a considerable body of literature, both ancient and contemporary, that discusses "fasting."

Each of us must find our own patterns of identifying with the poor. But there are many things that can be done by way of bringing ourselves to a point where we can begin to engage in intelligent action.

What is the role of the institutional churches in dealing with issues of poverty and oppression?

My primary focus in this discussion is on the laity as they carry out their mission outside the walls of the institutional church. Insofar as the church enters the picture here, then, it will be in relationship to the mission of the laity. But, of course, the laity do bear some responsibility for the integrity of the church. So we can at least mention the fact that the institutional church is, among other things, a corporate consumer, an employer, an investor, and a property owner. As these roles bear on the plight of the poor, the church's record has not always been a noble one. The church has been, on many occasions, a wasteful consumer, a discriminatory employer, an irresponsible investor, and a negligent property owner. We would all do well to keep a watchful eye on the patterns of church economics.

There is much that the church can do by way of enabling the laity to carry out a more effective ministry with regard to the poor. The pulpit has the potential for being an important agent of consciousness-raising in this area. Ordained ministers do not have to be experts in economics or politics in order to keep the full demands of the gospel before the laity. Church education programs, missionary groups, couples clubs, and the like also constitute an existing network for laity education and mission in this area of concern.

8

Equipping Laity for Ministry

THE PEOPLE of God—of whom the overwhelming majority are laity—have a mission to carry out in the world. This mission must include the corporate patterns of human life within its scope. An important theme in the Bible's mandate to God's people in the world is the call to perform "good works" in the larger society of which we are a part. The performance of these good works must include efforts on behalf of justice, righteousness, and peace. They must also have, as a central focus, the concerns of the poor and the oppressed.

These are some of the matters we have been discussing. But how can we bring these concerns to bear more directly on the actual life and self-understanding of the people of God today? How can we mobilize the Christian laity for the broad and complex mission we have been describing? What resources must we develop? What kinds of discussions and experiments can we encourage and promote? How can we make the present patterns of church life more supportive of the callings of lay persons?

Accepting the Difficulties

One thing we must *not* do is to ignore the genuine difficulties faced by the laity today as they seek to be faithful and effective servants of Jesus in the larger society. Indeed, acknowledging these difficulties is a crucial first step in the direction of faithful discipleship.

When I was a high school student, I belonged to a group of Christian teenagers who met regularly to discuss issues having to do with the Christian faith. At one of our meetings we were addressed by an alumna of our group who was home from college. She talked about some of the challenges and temptations she had experienced as a

Christian on a secular college campus. "But it's really wonderful being a Christian," she told us. "Jesus makes things so easy! If I weren't a Christian, I would have a lot of questions and problems; but as a Christian I know that Christ is the answer."

I never forgot those words. But I cannot say that they were a source of encouragement and assurance to me. In fact, those sentiments troubled me during my own studies in college and beyond. I have never found it "easy" to be a Christian. Indeed, I find the Christian life to be an immensely difficult venture. Unlike that young woman, I have always felt that I must struggle with difficult challenges and questions posed to me as a Christian. And I have never felt that being a Christian made easy answers available to me.

Indeed, there have even been times when I have felt that it might be "easier" *not* to be a Christian. I can illustrate this from the work I do in the area of political theory. Recently, I read a book on political theory—a rather standard work on the subject—in which, early in his discussion, the author asked, "Why is man political?" and proceeded to give a two-paragraph answer to the question. As a Christian I was more puzzled by the question itself than the author seemed to be. It immediately occurred to me that Christians cannot accept the unqualified reference to "man" in the question. We believe that human beings were created in God's image for a life of service in the original creation. But human beings have rebelled against God; they have chosen to pursue their own sinful designs, both in their personal lives and in the corporate patterns of human interaction. In the midst of that fallen and broken situation God has offered pardon and grace in the person of his son, Jesus. Those who have accepted that offer of redemption are presently in the process of being released from the grip of sin on human life. Furthermore, they look forward to the promise summarized by the Apostle John: "Beloved, we are God's children now; it does not yet appear what we shall be, but we know that when he appears we shall be like him, for we shall see him as he is" (1 John 3:2).

With this overall scheme in mind it is very difficult to talk, in many contexts, simply about "man." This seems to hold for the discussion about politics. Why are human beings political? Before we can answer the question, we must first get clear about what manifestation or condition of human nature we are talking about. Are we asking why human beings as God originally *created* them are, or ought to be, political? Are we talking about what needs or functions politics serves under *sinful* conditions? Are we talking about whether or how *redeemed* people are political? Are we talking about how politics might be necessary for the citizens of the *new age* God has promised for his creation?

This is an example in which I as a Christian scholar am forced to introduce complexities into a question that for many non-Christians is a perfectly straightforward one. These same complexities enter into other areas of our lives. The attempt to bring our lives into conformity with biblical standards of behavior means that we as Christians have concerns and obligations—in our family lives, our sexual attitudes, our moral sensitivities—that will seem odd, and even outdated, to many of our fellow citizens in a pluralistic society. Yet we believe we ought not to compromise our standards under social pressure to conform. Yet we view these standards as intimately related to a *personal* commitment to the gospel of Christ. We want to acknowledge them in our families, in our interpersonal relationships, even in our business dealings and political activity. But we want to live out these commitments in such a manner that we are not simply forcing others to live and act in a way that is not consistent with their own basic values. Or we want to witness to others about our Christian faith without somehow manipulating them.

These matters are often difficult to work through. Sometimes it seems that life would be so much easier, so much less complex, if we could somehow blend our own patterns of behavior into contemporary mores and life-styles. But we know that this will not do. We know that we are called, not to live in conformity with the present sinful order, but to be transformed into agents who do the will of God.

To stress these difficulties is not to imply that the slogan "Christ is the answer" is without positive meaning for our lives. In a very profound sense the ultimate answers to the problems of life are to be found only by submitting to the Lordship of Jesus. But to opt for the Christian "answer" is not to choose an easy way. Indeed, in a very profound sense Jesus is also the questioner. He makes us uneasy. He prods us to look into problem areas. He continually thrusts new challenges and questions into our paths.

"Take my yoke upon you, and learn from me . . . my yoke is easy, and my burden is light'' (Matt. 11:29–30). These words, which Jesus spoke to his disciples, tell the complex story. Living the Christian life is to take an "easy yoke" on ourselves. In one sense it *is* a yoke. It makes life difficult. The Christian life is not burden-free. But in a profound sense it is an *easy* yoke. The easiness does not consist in the fact that the choice of discipleship eliminates complexity and puzzlement. Rather, the easiness resides in the assurance that there is a purpose to the struggle, that the way of discipleship leads to a victorious goal. "In the world you have tribulation"—a realistic assessment of the Christian's lot—"but be of good cheer, I have overcome the world" (John 16:33).

Recognizing Our Weakness

It is no act of superficial piety to insist that we must recognize our inadequacy for the task that is posed for us as Christians. We have already insisted that, biblically speaking, God's heart goes out to the cries of the helpless ones. The realization of our own "prop-less-ness," then, is a crucial element in preparing ourselves to be the people of God, ministering in the world.

In certain strands of Protestantism, there is a strong emphasis on the need for periodic "revivals" in the church. Unfortunately, this kind of emphasis has often been associated with emotionalism and an "otherworldly" brand of spirituality. Quite apart from the inadequacies often associated with prayers for revival, however, the fundamental desire for spiritual renewal in the Christian community is proper, and even laudable. The need for such an emphasis is especially obvious in the face of efforts to get the laity "involved" in social action and the like without a concern for spiritual renewal.

The mobilization of the laity for efforts in "holy worldliness" must be rooted in a spiritual renewal, in "revival." At other points in our discussion in this book we have already talked about the need to link together the "personal" and the "corporate" dimensions of the Christian life. But the theme bears repeating here. The ministries of the laity within the corporate structures of society must be grounded in a vibrant, living relationship with Jesus Christ as *personal* Savior and Lord. I do not think that we have been served well by those Christian thinkers who have insisted that the "social" dimensions of the gospel are more important than "personal piety." The truth of the matter is—or so I view things—that a commitment to the social dimensions of the gospel must be undergirded by patterns of personal piety.

This is not to say that I have a clear view as to where the "personal" leaves off and the "social" begins. It is perhaps better to speak of some matters being *more* personal than other matters, or some concerns being *more* social than others. But however we formulate the case, our corporate involvements seem to require a grounding in a personal commitment to Christ. We cannot expect people to trust the power of the gospel as it bears on wars among nations until they have experienced the gospel as a power that touches the wars that go on within their own souls. We cannot speak with credibility about the complex temptations that are experienced at the centers of corporate power if we have not dealt with the temptations that threaten our lives as individuals. We are not ready to witness to a divine peace that can reach across cultural and ethnic barriers if we have not experienced the peace that passes human understanding as it touches our relationships with our immediate neighbors.

The mobilization of the laity for ministry in the world cannot take place apart from a concern with personal commitment to the claims of the gospel. As Christian laity we must recognize our own weakness. We must examine the patterns of our past and present failure to measure up to the demands of discipleship. We must repent and beg for divine mercy and forgiveness. We must cultivate an openness to the power of the gospel at the personal centers of our lives. And we must face the implications of our Christian callings with the assurance that God is faithful to his promise that his power will be made perfect in our weakness (1 Cor. 12:9).

Education for Lay Ministries

Suppose all the Christian laity were convinced that they needed to engage in ministries within the corporate structures of society. Suppose all of them were aware of their own shortcomings and weaknesses in relation to those ministries. Suppose all the Christian laity repented of sin and failure, pleaded for the mercies of God, and cultivated hearts of openness to the leading of the Spirit in their lives.

There would still be considerable work to do in order to prepare them for effective ministries in the world. Not the least of the outstanding needs would be for programs of laity education, aimed at equipping the laity for Christian service.

There are, of course, existing programs of laity education. This is not an area that has been completely neglected by the Christian community. Adult Sunday school classes; Christian service organizations; groups of lay persons who are organized along various occupational lines; organizations for married couples and singles; orientation programs for church officers—all of these contribute something to the task of laity education. But, even considered altogether, such programs as presently constituted are woefully inadequate to meet the challenges of lay ministry.

For one thing, these programs are extremely meager when compared to the kind of education that is offered to—even demanded of—the ordained clergy. Many denominations invest huge amounts of money in the education of clergy: they establish and maintain theological schools, pay the salaries of faculty and staff, subsidize tuition, and provide scholarships—all aimed at producing well-educated clergy. In any given year the actual dollar amounts spent by many denominations for the education of the clergy easily exceed the amounts allocated for laity education. When we consider the fact that the clergy constitute a very small percentage of denominational membership, the imbalance is shocking.

Furthermore, existing laity education programs are often poorly staffed and poorly planned. The "faculty" for such programs are often poorly equipped "volunteer" lay persons or overworked clergy. In many of the contexts mentioned, educational goals are subordinate to other purposes and functions—fellowship, "service," entertainment, organizational "business."

And even where there is a clear commitment to *educational* goals, the topics treated have very little to do with the corporate involvements of the laity. I once talked to a businessman who had just returned from a seminar held for Christian members of the business community. He had traveled to a distant city to hear lectures on "Bible Prophecy and the Modern State of Israel." From his enthusiastic report it was obvious that no attention at all was paid to the question of how Christians ought to function in the worlds of banking, insurance, or food processing. Other laity education programs deal primarily with family issues, evangelism aids, Bible study, and church doctrine.

None of this is bad or unimportant (although I have my own theological doubts about "Israel in Prophecy" discussions). A comprehensive program in laity education will attend to many of these items. But no such program is comprehensive unless it also addresses the patterns of laity involvement within the corporate structures. Laity education must deal with questions about what the Christian faith means for daily Christian involvement in the world.

How can we begin to correct this situation? One place to start is in the pulpit. The clergy can perform an important service in the area of laity education by promoting an awareness of the fundamentals of "laity theology." We must not expect that the ordained ministry will perform the whole task of laity education, but the clergy can see to it that there is an awareness of the *importance* of the task. It is crucial that the call to involvement in the mission of God's people in the world be announced and explained to congregations gathered for worship.

We can put the case this way: at the very least the clergy are responsible for making the laity aware of the fact that there *is* a mandate for corporate obedience to the gospel, even if the clergy themselves are not the ones to spell out the *how* of that mission.

In seminars I have conducted for clergy and seminary students, I have often heard a complaint of this sort: "You want us to preach and teach about politics. But we simply have no expertise in that area. How can we preach sermons on subjects about which we know very little?" This question betrays a misunderstanding of the role of the clergy in this area. It is not necessary for the clergy to be experts in political, military, and economic affairs to articulate the fact that the gospel makes claims in these areas. It takes no special economic expertise to preach a sermon developing the theme that the God of the Scriptures cares about the poor and the oppressed. It doesn't take a degree in political science to prepare a sermon in which Christians are encouraged to scrutinize the issues in a given electoral campaign in the light of biblical concerns. It takes no special military expertise to demonstrate that the God and Father of Jesus Christ has no use for sword-rattling militarism or appeals to the nationalistic pride of citizens of "the greatest nation on the face of the earth."

Sermons dealing with such themes will, of course, leave the laity with many questions. Who *are* the poor and oppressed today? Who are the "widows" and "orphans" and "sojourners" of our contemporary world? How much of the opposition to government bureau-cracies, and the budget-cutting sentiments, among today's electo-rates are attributable to self-interest, as opposed to a genuine concern for "good stewardship"? Under what conditions can one nation engage in military action against another? How shall we evaluate actual arguments for and against the stockpiling of nuclear weapons?

These are not questions that must be decided in the pulpit. These are questions that the people of God must struggle with as they seek to bring the claims of the gospel, which they hear articulated in the pulpit, to bear on their political decision-making.

Similarly, the clergy do not have to give detailed lectures on multi-national corporations, trade with the Soviet Union, health care plans, advertising practices, guidelines for the small business, school budgets, and so on. But they can make it clear that these are matters that must be addressed with Christian sensitivities by the laity.

Efforts must also be made to gain for the clergy a more contex-tualized understanding of the ways in which urgent practical issues arise in the lives of lay people. One way to accomplish this is by creating situations in which clergy can be taught by lay people about the actual tensions and dilemmas that emerge in the course of "worldly" ministries. Another is for clergy periodically to visit places of employment and commerce for extended periods of observation. Perhaps priests or ordained ministers should even be granted sabbati-cal leaves for the purpose of spending several months in insurance offices or factories or supermarkets.

But how can we better facilitate the creative struggles of the laity with regard to their daily ministries? In order to do this, we must find ways of bridging the gap between the general mandate to engage in mission that goes forth from the pulpit (when it is functioning prop-erly) and the very practical, and often lonely, activities of the laity in their daily callings.

This is an area that requires much imagination. Furthermore, it is extremely important that the planning of programs for laity education draw on the sensitivities of the laity. Lay people must be involved in the designing and implementing of the programs, on a leadership level.

One good place to begin is with the present structures of laity education. We have already mentioned some of these: church education programs, couples' and singles' clubs, organizations for Christians in the business world, and other occupationally oriented groups, service organizations, political action groups. With the proper concerns and sensitivities, these can be important vehicles for delivering educational opportunities to the laity.

Laity Attitudes

These programs will be effective, however, only if the participants are lay people who have, or are in the process of developing, certain characteristics. First, we need lay persons who are firmly convinced of the corporate calling of the people of God. They must sense the mandate and be willing to engage in the process of being educated to fulfill that mandate effectively.

Second, we need lay persons who are willing to explore the difficult questions of how the gospel relates to various occupations and professions. This is an area in which there is a desperate need to go beyond general talk about "theology of the laity." It is important that we develop theological perspectives on business activity, medical care, food services, bureaucratic patterns, tourism and recreation, and so on. Guidelines for these specific areas of corporate action cannot be developed *for* the laity. They must be developed *by* the laity.

In my own Reformed tradition great emphasis has often been placed on viewing one's occupation—whatever that occupation may be—as a "Christian vocation." An important implication of this emphasis is that, given any occupation, there is a uniquely Christian way to carry out one's duties with regard to that area of activity. I am convinced of the profundity of this perspective. But it is not without its difficulties, especially as we move beyond rhetoric to the actual realities of daily work. In what way can Christian commitment affect the activities of the postal carrier, the bank teller, the waitress, the florist, the truck driver?

To pursue these questions properly, a third characteristic is necessary: the laity must approach these questions with utter candor and an openness to self-examination. I must make a candid observation at this point. I have been involved in a number of conferences and symposia where Christians from both the business world and the academic community have come together for dialogue on contemporary social issues. In such situations I have had the impression that Christians who work for large business corporations seldom sound any different than their fellow employees who are not Christians. At the same time I have often been convinced that Christian academics often approach such dialogues with an equally "ideological" mentality. The result is that conversations of that sort seldom go any further, nor are they characterized by a different spirit, than comparable discussions among persons who are not Christians. There is a crucial need for Christians to approach these issues in a spirit of willingness to examine honestly their own vested interests and party lines in the light of the claims of the gospel.

The New Mission Field

In a speech given at the 1971 Jerusalem Conference on Biblical Prophecy, James M. Houston called on Christians "to use the whole range of their professional skills to speak prophetically about our times, [reaching] into every area of professional life, just as in the past we have emphasized the geographical penetration of the world with the Gospel." Dr. Houston's comparison here of the Christian mandate with regard to various professions with the missionary calling is an illuminating one.

Just as in the past we have emphasized the geographical spread of the gospel, so now we must emphasize the professional spread of the gospel. This is not the place to evaluate various criticisms that have been lodged in recent years against the missionary movement that was so dominant in the nineteenth century and that extends into our present time. Suffice it to say that the missionary enterprise has not been without mistakes and weaknesses, but it has also provided us with some very noble examples of dedication to the gospel. Missionaries have often left home and kindred, at great personal sacrifice, to go into uncharted territories, motivated by the conviction that the gospel must be spread to the ends of the earth.

This is the kind of dedication and conviction that must come to characterize the laity movement in our own time. We must view the vast array of contemporary structures and institutions, occupations and professions, vocations and avocations as a mission field of sorts. We must understand Christ's command to go into the "whole world" as pointing not only to the diversity of languages and cultures that we view from some distance, but also to the social, political, and economic worlds in which we regularly traffic but that often seem far removed from the influence of justice and righteousness.

Missionaries in the nineteenth century ventured into what were for them uncharted continents, armed only with the confidence that there are no cattle on any of a thousand distant hills that have not been formed by the Creator's hand and that there is no human being in any jungle compound who is not created in the image of the God who has revealed his will in Jesus Christ. Similarly, we as Christian laity must participate in the complex worlds of business, medicine, law, entertainment, and government with the full confidence that there is no economic or political sin for which the Lamb of God is not a worthy sacrifice and that there is no dark or dusty corner of industry or education that falls outside the scope of the gospel's power.

And we must carry out this assignment with the zeal and spirit of self-sacrifice that have been typical of much of the "foreign missions" enterprise. For those who have been willing to follow through on their Christian commitment, no matter what the cost, the goal has never been simply success or personal happiness or "worldly acclaim." The goal has been that of obedience itself, in the knowledge that the God who gives the mandate to act obediently is also the one who sent his own son into the world, not to condemn the world, but that the world might be saved through him.

The Call of Jesus to Holy Worldliness
(A Concluding Meditation)

> *And they were filled with awe, and said to one another, "Who then is this, that even wind and sea obey him?"*
>
> —Mark 4:41

THE FOLLOWERS of Jesus are called to holy worldliness. This has been the constant theme of our discussion thus far. As the people of God we are required to participate in a divinely mandated mission in the world that God created.

We will conclude our discussion here on a "devotional" note. In the above text the disciples of Jesus reacted with wonder at an exhibition of Jesus' power over the forces of nature. His demonstration of his authority over the angry sea caught them by surprise. But they began to see something of the scope of his redemptive mission as the one who came to reclaim a world in the grip of sin. They began to see that Jesus is a "worldly" Lord. And as the early church reflected on the Lordship of Jesus, they came to realize that they were called to participate in the worldly mission of Jesus. And so are we.

Who Is Jesus?

In the Old Testament the encounters between God and the forces of chaos that threaten God's ordering, creating purposes are often depicted in terms of a struggle between God's power and the furor of mighty waves and waters. Such an encounter is portrayed graphically in Psalm 93, one of the royal psalms:

The floods have lifted up, O Lord,
the floods have lifted up their voice,
the floods lift up their roaring.
Mightier than the thunders of many waters,
mightier than the waves of the sea,
the Lord on high is mighty.

It is likely that, in singing this hymn, the thoughts of the people of Israel turned to the story of creation, with its account of God's ordering the chaotic waters; to the account of the great flood, when God called forth the fountains of the deep in order to bring destruction on a rebellious race; to the Exodus event, when the parting of the waters meant deliverance for Israel and the collapse of the watery walls brought judgment on Israel's pursuers. There exist, side by side in the Old Testament, stories of miraculous gifts of water to nations and individuals on the one hand and, on the other hand, visions—as in the Book of Daniel—of the angry sea spewing forth raging beasts who are bent on destruction.

And then, on a certain day "when evening had come," our Lord and his disciples were in a boat crossing the lake. A storm came upon them, and the waves threatened to destroy their craft. Jesus, awakened by the disciples, rose to rebuke the wind and the sea. Immediately, we are told, everything became calm.

Any group of human beings would surely have greeted this turn of events with considerable surprise. But we can imagine the marvel of the disciples, who were, after all, Jews with Old Testament sensitivities. They knew that God alone has power over angry waves and mighty winds. This knowledge could not have been far from their minds as they turned in awe to each other, asking "Who then is this, that even wind and sea obey him?"

"Who is this Jesus?" This is a question that was to be asked many times during Jesus' lifetime. It was asked, in one form or another, by the teachers in the temple when he visited there as a boy, by the citizens of Jesus' hometown when he returned there during his public ministry, by various folks who heard him preach or who experienced his healing power, by Nicodemus, by Pilate, and by many others. After his death and resurrection it was to be asked again many times—by friends who walked with him, unknowingly, on the road to Emmaus, by Saul as he cried out in the direction of the light that had blinded him, and even by the writer of the book of Revelation—who, tradition tells us, had been his beloved disciple but who fell to the ground as one who was dead when he saw the glorified Christ on the Isle of Patmos.

"Who is this Jesus?" This is a question many are still asking today. The question is even being asked by many who claim to have known Jesus well in the past. At the very beginning of this book I told of an oilman who is in the process of discovering that Jesus has concerns that make it impossible for this man to continue in an uncritical acceptance of his past economic attitudes. Recently, a teacher of an adult Sunday school class told me of a class member who, after several weeks of detailed class discussion of the economic and political perspectives of the gospel accounts, exclaimed in anguish: "I have thought for a long time that I knew Jesus personally—but now I feel as if he is a stranger to me."

These lay people, and many others, are having an experience similar to that of the disciples. They had accustomed themselves to thinking of Jesus in very familiar terms. Then something happened to surprise them. Suddenly, Jesus seems to be an unfamiliar figure—a stranger.

Talking about Jesus

In his collection of sermons, *The Shaking of the Foundations,* Paul Tillich offers some interesting reflections on Peter's confession in Mark 8. Tillich notes that Peter's stirring confession regarding Jesus, "Thou art the Christ," is followed by a puzzling observation by the writer of the gospel account: "And [Jesus] charged them to tell no one about him." But the point of Jesus' warning soon becomes clear. When Jesus goes on to tell the disciples that the Son of man must suffer at the hands of the authorities and must be killed by them, Peter rebukes him. Peter does not think that Jesus should have to suffer and die; he does not properly understand the mission of the one whom he has identified as "the Christ."

Tillich observes that it may be that if Jesus were to speak directly to the church today, he would also charge *us* not to tell anyone about him. This is a shocking suggestion in a day in which great emphasis is placed on evangelism, on "telling others about Jesus." But the suggestion ought not to be ignored. "Evangel" means "good news," and there can be no doubt that we are called to "evangelize"; we are commissioned to be bearers of the good news. To take Tillich's suggestion seriously is not to detract from the importance of this commission. Indeed, it is precisely because the commission is of such great importance that we ought to consider seriously the possibility that Jesus might well try to silence the church today.

We are not called to say just anything that happens to come into our heads about Jesus. It is not our job to speak loosely or flippantly or imprecisely about him. We are called to proclaim *the* good news. The gospel has a specific and rich content. To distort or to trivialize that message is a serious matter. Consequently, we must be constantly returning to gaze on, to reflect on, to reconsider, the one who commissions us to speak in his name. We must constantly ask the question, "Who is this?"

Unfortunately, we lay Christians have not always been willing to engage in that process of reflection and renewal. We have not always been willing to explore the full dimensions of a proper answer to the question, "Who is Jesus?" We have often preferred to have the gospel reduced to simple formulas and clichés; we have preferred to trim the person and ministry of Jesus down to a "manageable" size.

The proper alternative to these all-too-frequent patterns is to permit ourselves to stand in awe before the complex and puzzling Jesus of the gospels. To do so is to encounter a Jesus who does not always conform to our expectations. When Jesus stilled the angry waves, he was doing more than bolstering his reputation as a Savior of individual souls. He was not engaging in a bit of preevangelistic gimmickry. He was not attempting to attract the attention of his audience, in order suddenly to pounce on them with "four spiritual laws." He was not offering an object lesson in "possibility thinking" or "positive thinking."

When Jesus commanded the waves to be still, he was exhibiting his power as the Lord of creation, come to redeem a fallen world from the grip of sin. He was exercising the authority described so triumphantly in Isaac Watt's carol: "He comes to make his blessings flow/ far as the curse is found/ far as the curse is found!"

Jesus directly confronted the complex cursedness of the creation. The Gospel of Mark, in which this version of the story is found, also portrays Jesus as casting out demons, forgiving sins, healing broken bodies, changing the economic attitudes of tax collectors, and even raising the dead. And over and over again, those who witnessed these deeds asked: "Who then is this?"

Jesus conducted a cosmic mission. He was not, and is not, merely a personal Savior, or a therapist, or a healer, or a social critic, or a victor over demons and death—although he is surely at least each of these things. But he is also all of them and more. His mission was as large as the creation. His redeeming power reaches to wherever the curse is found. He has come to rescue the entire cosmos, in all its dimensions and activities, from the bonds of sin.

Passive and Active

The people of God—of whom the vast majority are laity—must relate to that cosmic mission of Jesus in at least two ways. First, we must give evidence that we are a community of persons who are ourselves *experiencing* the healing, calming, reconciling work of Jesus. This is the "passive" dimension of the relationship. We must be acted *upon* by the power of Jesus.

Our lives need to be calmed. We need to hear the word of peace. We are threatened by the forces of chaos and destruction. All around us we see evil at work, and our lives too are touched by disintegration and death, as described in the hymn:

> Christian, dost thou see them on the holy ground,
> How the powers of darkness rage thy steps around? . . .
>
> Christian, dost thou feel them, how they work within,
> Striving, tempting, luring, goading into sin?

The forces of chaos are at work in politics, in academia, in the worlds of business, entertainment, and the arts. They threaten marriages and schools, churches and nations, basketball teams and neighborhood associations.

But Jesus has entered into his creation in order to reclaim it. He successfully challenges those forces that threaten to pervert and distort all those things the Creator once pronounced "good." Because Jesus is in our midst, the forces of evil are doomed. And as Christians we experience that power. We sense the victory in a personal way. We know Jesus as one who brings peace to troubled lives. His power is present in our very personal struggles and dealings. But it is also a presence we know and celebrate communally, as a people whom God has visited as Savior and healer.

Second, we are called to *promote* his healing work in the world. Having experienced the firstfruits of his healing mission, we must *become* vehicles of his power in the larger society. This is the "active" dimension of the relationship. Having been acted *upon* by divine grace, we become *agents* of that grace.

The disciples who stood in awe of the mighty deeds of Jesus became, in the book of Acts, performers of mighty deeds, which caused others to stand in awe of *them,* asking, "Who are these people?" The transition comes in the words Jesus speaks to his disciples in John 20:21: "As the Father has sent me, even so I send you." The disciples become apostles. The ones who are acted upon become the agents. And so it is with us. We who have seen the power of Jesus become instruments of that power. We who have stood in awe become practitioners of the awesome.

This is not to suggest that we can divide these two dimensions into neatly separated time segments. It is not as if the disciples were, for a time, acted upon by Jesus, only to enter into a period in which they were forevermore "pure" agents of his power. They had to return frequently to the posture of observers and receivers of God's grace in Christ. And so must we. We—all of us—must be acting while we are being acted upon. We must be continually giving while we are at the same time receiving. We must be healers who are still in the process of being healed.

"All Things Hold Together"

We have paid much attention in these pages to the calling of the laity to act as agents of the power of Jesus. It is fitting that in these final comments we draw attention to the supreme importance of knowing who it is we serve. The writer to the Hebrews tells us that Jesus "reflects the glory of God and bears the very stamp of his [God's] nature, upholding the universe by his word of power" (Heb. 1:3). All things are "upheld" by Jesus. As Paul puts it in Colossians 1:17, "in him all things hold together."

We are called to demonstrate this fact in word and deed. It is our task to show, in the variety of areas in which we have been placed as servants of Jesus, that everything is held together by him. This is not a simple task. It is not easy to see how healing is possible in the business world or in academia or entertainment. It is not even easy at times to see how things can hold together in our families or in our own private streams of consciousness. But we have the assurance that the power of Jesus is a cohesive and pervasive power. And we can begin to experience that power as a healing force in our own lives and in the activities in which we engage.

It is important to keep in mind that in this area we are dealing with "firstfruits" and "signs" of the new order. By uttering the word of "peace," Jesus did not forevermore silence the raging seas. Demons still work their destruction in individual lives and corporate entities. Human bodies are still wracked with disease and pain. Tax collectors and centurions still collaborate in deeds of oppression.

The mighty deeds Jesus performed during his earthly ministry were meant as initial signs of a full transformation that is yet in the future. The unified rule of Jesus is not yet universally obvious. By faith we know that the full victory will come someday, when Jesus announces: "Behold, I make all things new. . . . It is done! I am the Alpha and the Omega, the beginning and the end" (Rev. 21:5–6). The knowledge that the final victory is, in fact, coming can provide us with the goal toward which we must presently work.

But our own present efforts must also deal in "signs" and "first-fruits." We are not called to transform the world completely here and now. If that were our goal, we would still have to be very realistic about the ways in which our sin and finitude touch all our efforts. But we are not even called to transform the world. Rather, it is our task to live and act in such a way that our deeds point to the final victory.

Agents of Victory

There are many ways in which we can function presently as agents of the kingdom that has not yet arrived in its fullness. We can become ever more conscious of our identity as God's people. We can antici-pate the new order in worship and work. We can seek to bring the demands of the gospel to bear increasingly on our individual lives and corporate involvements. God does not ask us to be "messiahs," but he does call us to be fully committed to the effort of becoming faithful servants of Jesus.

"Who then is this?" There is a legitimate note of surprise in this question of the disciples. Such surprise ought not to be absent from our own asking of the question. The kingdom of Jesus is full of surprises. We should be constantly surprised by the ways and places in which the power of the gospel shows up in our lives: in our roles as consumers and partygoers; in the classroom, the bedroom, the pasture, and the playground.

But our obligations do not end at that point where we are surprised by the wonders of the kingdom of Jesus. We must in turn be sources of surprise to the unbelieving world. We should be thinking and speaking and acting in ways that invite the disciples' question in forms appropriate for our day: "Who then is this? Who are these people who attend to broken lives and bodies, who reconcile enemies, who promote justice and love mercy, who sanctify business dealings and overturn racial and cultural barriers? By whose power do they act?"

> Dost ask who that may be? Christ Jesus, it is he . . . .
> The prince of darkness grim, we tremble not for him;
> His rage we can endure, for lo! his doom is sure,
> One little word shall fell him.
>   ("A Mighty Fortress Is Our God")

Jesus spoke one little word and the angry seas became calm. Someday he will speak that little word and it will be received by the whole creation as a final and decisive word of power.

The laity—the people of God who are called to minister in the broad reaches of God's creation—have also heard that little word as a word of peace in their own troubled lives. To those of us who have experienced his healing grace, he has given the power to be the agents of his cosmic mission of redemption. The exact shapes that our ministries must take—in the business sector, in politics, in the home, the school, the theater, and the hospital—will become discernible only as we commit ourselves to the effort. But the mandate is clear. And the final victory is promised.

Books and Articles Cited

Bellah, Robert. *The Broken Covenant: American Civil Religion in Time of Trial.* New York: Seabury Press, 1975.

Berger, Peter. *The Noise of Solemn Assemblies: Christian Commitment and the Religious Establishment in America.* Garden City: Doubleday, 1961.

Berkhof, Hendrik. *Christ and the Powers.* Scottdale, Pa.: Herald Press, 1962.

Borg, Marcus. *Conflict and Social Change.* Minneapolis: Augsburg Publishing House, 1971.

"The Boston Affirmations." *Worldview,* March 1976.

Calvin, John. *Institutes of the Christian Religion.* Ed. John T. McNeill. Philadelphia: Westminster Press, Library of Christian Classics, 1960.

Cassidy, Richard J. *Jesus, Politics, and Society: A Study of Luke's Gospel.* Maryknoll, N.Y.: Orbis Books, 1978.

De Klerk, W. A. *The Puritans in Africa: A Story of Afrikanerdom.* London, England: R. Collings, 1975.

Gibbs, Mark. *Christians with Secular Power.* Philadelphia: Fortress Press, Laity Exchange Books, 1981.

———, and Morton, T. Ralph. *God's Frozen People: A Book for and about Christian Laymen.* Philadelphia: Westminster Press, 1965.

Houston, James M. "The Judgment of the Nations," in *Prophecy in the Making: Messages Prepared for the Jerusalem Conference on Biblical Prophecy.* Ed. Carl F. H. Henry. Carol Stream, Ill.: Creation House, 1971.

Kraemer, Hendrik. *A Theology of the Laity.* London, England: Lutterworth Press, 1958.

Miller, Perry. *Errand into the Wilderness.* Cambridge, Mass.: Harvard University Press, 1956.

de Santa Ana, Julio. *Good News to the Poor: The Challenge of the Poor in the History of the Church.* Maryknoll, N.Y.: Orbis Books, 1979.

Sider, Ronald. *Rich Christians in an Age of Hunger: A Biblical Study.* Downers Grove, Ill.: Inter-varsity Press, 1977.

Smedes, Lewis. "From Hartford to Boston." *The Reformed Journal,* April 1976.

Tillich, Paul. *The Shaking of the Foundations*. New York: Charles Scribner's Sons, 1948.

Yoder, John Howard. "Exodus and Exile: The Two Faces of Liberation." *Cross Currents,* Fall 1973.